Henry Green, Robert Wigram

Chronicles of Blackwall Yard

Part I.

Henry Green, Robert Wigram

Chronicles of Blackwall Yard
Part I.

ISBN/EAN: 9783337020552

Printed in Europe, USA, Canada, Australia, Japan

Cover: Foto ©ninafisch / pixelio.de

More available books at **www.hansebooks.com**

CHRONICLES

BLACKWALL YARD.

PART I.

BY

HENRY GREEN AND ROBERT WIGRAM.

"*Nos . . . . nec gravem*
Pelidæ stomachum, cedere nescii,
Nec cursus duplicis per mare Ulixei,
Nec sævam Pelopis domum
Conamur, tenues grandia : .   .   .
                              Hor., Lib. I., Car. IV.

PUBLISHED BY WHITEHEAD, MORRIS AND LOWE.

1881.

Chronicles of Blackwall Yard.

Chapter I.

A T the time when our Chronicles commence, the Hamlet of Poplar and Blackwall, in which the dockyard whose history we propose to sketch is situated, was, together with the Hamlets of Ratcliffe and Mile End, included in the old Parish of Stebunhethe, now Stepney, in the hundred of Ossulston. The Manor of Stebunhethe is stated in the Survey of Doomsday to have been parcel of the ancient demesnes of the Bishopric of London. It is there described as of large extent, and valued at £48 per annum! In the year 1299 a Parliament was held by King Edward I., at Stebunhethe, in the house of Henry Walleis, Mayor of London, when that monarch confirmed the charter of liberties. Stebunhethe Marsh adjoining to Blackwall, which was subsequently called the South Marsh, but now the Isle of Dogs, was some years after this described as a tract of land lying within the curve which the Thames forms between Ratcliffe and Blackwall. Continual reference is made in local records to the embankments of this marsh, and to the frequent breaches in them. In an inquisition taken in the reign of Edward II. relating to the repairs of the embankments of Stebunhethe Marsh, it is stated that a former Lord of the Manor had recovered 100 acres of land from the river " by making of banks and ditches, which, when neglected to be repaired were liable to be overflown ;" that the same lord afterwards granted 42½ acres of this land in parcels to his freemen, and the residue to his bondmen, each person being required to repair the banks upon his own land. It appears that the freemen had done what was requisite on their parts, but that the bondmen had suffered the banks upon their lands to go to decay, in consequence of which they and the Bishop of London (as Lord of the Manor) were by the Sheriff of the County required to repair them, which was done accordingly.

1067.

1299.
Lyson's En-
virons,
p. 678.
Stow's
Annals.
p. 319.

1307.
Edward II.

1324.   Soon afterwards, in the year 1324, a great flood happened, which caused a breach upon the land of one of the Bishop's tenants near Shadwell, when a question arose whether the expense of this repair should fall only on the landowner where the breach happened, or whether the other proprietors of marsh land within the Manor should be obliged to join in bearing the expense. The matter came to a trial and was determined in favour of the Bishop's tenant, as may be seen more at large in "Dugdale on Draining and Embanking," where is an account of several commissions for viewing and repairing the banks of Stebunhethe Marsh.

In this Marsh stood an ancient chapel called the Chapel of St. Mary in Stepney Marsh. It is mentioned by that name in a will of the 15th century. The object of its foundation does not appear. It is not likely that the Marsh could at that time have had many inhabitants. Perhaps it was a hermitage founded by some devout person for the purpose of saying masses for the souls of mariners. In 1821 this Chapel had been converted into a neat farm-house, standing upon the same foundation, and was then the only dwelling place upon the Marsh. It is described as exhibiting no remains of antiquity, except in the lower parts of the walls which are built of small stones and flints. A Gothic window was removed about the year 1790.

1351.   In the 24th year of Edward III., Sir John de Pulteney, an eminent citizen of London, who had been four times Lord Mayor, and was founder of Pulteney College, died seized of the Manor of Popeler (now Poplar). This Sir John de Pulteney is said to have lived in a quaint old house, still existing in Coldharbour at Blackwall, nearly opposite to the well-known "Artichoke" Tavern. In this same house it is also said that the celebrated discoverer Sebastian Cabot lived some years afterwards, when he is described as having been in "strict correspondence with Sir Thomas Pert, Vice-Admiral of England, who had a house at Popeler, and promised Sebastian Cabot a good ship of the King's in order to make discoveries." Tradition, further assigns the same house a few years later to no less a tenant than the great Sir Walter Raleigh.

1377.   The first distinct mention of Blackwall is, we are told, to be found in an old record of 1377, when J. Milend and others obtained a contract for embanking the river Thames at Blackwall.

1396.   In the year 1396, the reversion of the Manor of Popeler was granted after the death of Margaret, wife of Sir John Devereux, by William de Wickham, Bishop of Winchester, Sir Aubrey de Vere and others to the

Abbey of St. Mary de Graces, near the Tower of London. After the dissolution of monasteries, this Manor remained long vested in the Crown, and was among the Manors settled on Charles I. when Prince of Wales. By King Charles I. it was, in the fourth year of his reign, granted to certain persons, trustees for the city of London, by whom it was afterwards sold to Sir John Jacob. In 1558 it was conveyed by Bridget Gardye to Sir Francis Jopson, in 1583 by John Hampson to Thomas Fanshaw, by the latter in 1588 to Edward Elliott. In 1620 it was the property of John Wyllams, who obtained a fresh grant of it in that year; in 1637 he sold it to Robert Hooker. It has since passed through many private hands, and is now, we believe, the sole property of James Humphries, Esq.

Lands in this Manor descend according to the custom of gavel-kind.

The Manor House of Poplar has long been held separately from the demesne; it was formerly possessed and occupied by Sir Gilbert and Sir William Dethick, successively Garter King-at-arms, and it was still in the possession of the Dethick family in 1709.

The house, an ancient wooden building, was situated on the south side of the present East India Dock Road, but being in a very dilapidated state, it was partially re-built by Mrs. Wade in 1810, and is now in the occupation of Dr. F. M. Corner.

1515.   In the sixth year of the reign of King Henry VIII., who virtually was the founder of the English navy, and who established the Navy Office and the Royal Dockyards at Deptford, Woolwich, and Chatham, we find the following record from November 2nd, 1515, to the 20th of April in the following year:—"There was paid by John Hopton, then being Clerk Controller of all the King's Royal ships, &c., the cost of bringing the 'Mary George' from Blackwall to Barking, 17 shillings. The 'Mary George' being of portage 250—300 tons lyeth upon the south side of the Isle of Dogs, and must be caulked within the board and without; also she must be searched for worm holes, because she hath been in Levant. The 'Mary and John,' from Blackwall to Limehouse, 8 shillings."

Chapter II.

1587.   WE now come to the first mention of the scene of these Chronicles, which occurs in the twenty-ninth year of the reign of Queen Elizabeth—that is, in the year preceding the arrival of the Spanish Armada—when Henry, the third Lord Wentworth leased on November 1st for five hundred years to Roger

A 1

Richardson "a parcel of ground called Blackwall, extending from Poplar to the landing-place there, in length by estimation four hundred yards, and a parcel of waste ground, extending from the said landing place to a sluice towards the south-west, in length six hundred and fourteen yards," &c., &c. The above term was assigned by Roger Richardson to Nicholas Andrews, and it must have been during the tenure of either Richardson or Andrews that one of them, or possibly the first East India Company, which is supposed to have been in occupation of this property a few years later, commenced to lay out Blackwall Yard.

(*See title deeds.*)

At this time the greatest anxiety was experienced throughout the country with regard to the threatened invasion of the so-called "Invincible Armada," and among the various preparations that were made to check its progress, the following order was issued for the protection of the River Thames :—" The manner how the River of Thames shall be kept assured against any attempts of the galleys, by the care and good regard of Sir Henry Palmer, who is appointed to the charge of that service.

Charnock.

1. " First a pinnace to lie at Tilbury Hope, or in the best place thereabout ; this pinnace, upon the discovery of any galley, shall weigh and shoot her ordnance to give the alarm to the forts and 'Victory.' The 'Victory' to lie between the two forts of Gravesend and Tilbury, and that order be taken that certain of the inhabitants of the town of Gravesend and thereabout may be selected and appointed upon the alarm, to go with their furniture, in all possible speed, aboard the 'Victory' ; and that the barges and boats of the said town may set them on board the ship, albeit it be in the night. Upon which alarm, and certain view of the galleys, the said ships and forts are to shoot off their ordnance and give the alarm to the 'Lyon.' The 'Lyon' to ride about Greenhithe, there to receive the alarm from the 'Victory' and forts, and thereupon to send away up to the Court the row barge, with some discreet person to advertise, and also to give the alarm to those ships that ride at Blackwall, that they may prepare."

1588.

In 1588, a plan, now in the British Museum, entitled " Thamesis descriptio," by Robert Adams, surveyor of the buildings to Queen Elizabeth, was published. " On a small parchment roll, drawn with a pen, showing lines across the river to mark how far and from whence cannon-balls may obstruct the passage of any ship on an invasion, from Tilbury to London, with proper distances marked for placing the guns." This plan shows also a barrier, or stockade, across the river at Blackwall, but it is considered doubtful whether this was ever really carried out, although certain large piles running apparently across the river, which were discovered many years afterwards, when laying the foundations of a new graving-dock in Blackwall Yard, would appear to support the idea that it really was constructed. The fear of the Spanish Armada, and the successful enterprise of Sir Francis Drake had by this time aroused the energies of the country, and the force collected to resist the invasion amounted to 197 vessels of various descriptions, of the aggregate burden of nearly 30,000 tons.

At the beginning of the year 1600, the mercantile navy of England was reduced to a very low state, most of the commerce being carried on in foreign bottoms. The incitement offered by the advantageous trade in which the Dutch had long engaged to India, at length, however, moved the nation, and on the 31st December in this year, Elizabeth, at the solicitation of several great men and eminent merchants, granted to them an exclusive charter for fifteen years for the establishing of a commerce to the East Indies, thereby constituting them a body corporate, by the style of the Governor and Company of the Merchants of London trading to the East Indies. This Company is commonly known as the "First English East India Company." In consequence of this charter the Company lost no time in raising a Joint Stock for promoting their design of carrying their project immediately into execution, in which they were so successful as soon to find themselves masters of £72,000 (no small sum at that time); with this they determined to commence their trade, and gave beginning to it by fitting out five able ships for the first voyage to the Moluccas and Java, of which squadron the "Dragon" of 600 tons was admiral, the "Hector" of 300 tons was vice-admiral, the "Susannah" and "Ascension" of 200 tons each, and the "Guest," a store-ship of 130 tons burthen; the whole complement of men was 420, the expense of equipping them £45,000, and the remaining £27,000 of their cash was expended in the purchase of cargoes. They sailed from Torbay 2nd of May, 1601.

The formation of this East India Company was soon followed by the building at Woolwich, in 1603, of the largest ship that had yet been constructed for the purposes of commerce, at least in England; King James I., in whom the Company found a powerful protector, dined on board of her, and gave her the name of the "Trades Increase"; she is reported to have been of twelve hundred tons burthen. The king also named a pinnace of two hundred and fifty tons, that was built at the same time, the "Pepper-

marginal notes:
1589.

1600.

Formation of First East India Company.

1603.

corn." The impetus once having been given, before the end of the reign of King James an important mercantile navy was owned by British merchants.

1604. In 1604 the East India Company fitted out and despatched a second squadron of four ships, under the command of Sir Henry Middleton, for

1605. the Moluccas and Java. And in the following year, the growing interest that was felt throughout the country in all matters connected with ship building was further marked by the formation of the Shipwrights' Company.

1607. In 1607 the East India Company undertook a third expedition to the East with three ships only, which they successfully performed, especially in the Moluccas, and, though their treatment by the Dutch was very indifferent, yet they could not hinder these ships from procuring a valuable cargo of spice, which they brought safely to the Downs May 10th, 1610, " with this remarkable instance of Providence that in this whole voyage out and home they had not lost a single man."

1610. In 1610 we find the following description of "a most goodly ship for warre," built at Woolwich :—" The keel whereof was one hundred and fourteen feet long, and the cross beam was forty-four feet in length, she will carry sixty-four pieces of great ordnance, and is of the burden of fourteen hundred tons. This Royal ship is double built, and is most sumptuously adorned, within and without, with all manner of curious carving, painting, and rich gilding, being in all respects the greatest and goodliest ship that ever was built in England ; and this glorious ship the king gave unto his son, Henry Prince of Wales. The 24th of September the King, the Queen, the Prince of Wales, the Duke of York, and the Lady Elizabeth, with many great lords, went unto Woolwich to see it launcht ; but, because of the narrowness of the dock, it could not then be launcht. Whereupon the Prince came the next morning by three o'clock, and then, at the launching thereof, the Prince named it after his own dignity, and called it the ' Royal Prince.' The great workmaster in building this ship was Mr. Phineas Pett, gentleman, some time Master of Arts of Emmanuel College, in Cambridge," who continued Principal Engineer of the Navy during the reign of Charles II.

1612. In May, 1612, the Shipwrights' Company before alluded to was formally incorporated by a charter granted "to the Master, Wardens and Commonalty of the Art or Mystery of Shipwrights," the above-mentioned Mr. Phineas Pett being appointed the first Master.

It may here be stated that the family of the Petts had held the office of architects to the Royal Navy for two hundred years, and were the great instruments in the improvement of our ships of war. They modernized them by divesting all their vessels of a great deal of the cumbrous top hamper entailed on them from the castellated defences which had been necessary in, and which yet remained from, the hand-to-hand encounter of the middle ages; and it is probable that but for the taste for gorgeous decorations which prevailed during the seventeenth century this ingenious family would have been able to effect much more. As it was, they decidedly rendered England pre-eminently the school for naval architecture during the time they constructed its fleets.

The year 1612 is a most interesting and important date in the Chronicles of Blackwall Yard, or of the East India Yard, as it was then called, for in this year the Dwelling House and Offices, with probably the dry docks, storehouses, and other buildings were completed, a tablet on the inside wall above the gateway bore this date, while on the outside wall were placed the arms of the first East India Company. These arms heraldically described are: Azure three ships of three masts, rigged and under full sail, the sails, pennants, and ensigns argent, each charged with a cross gules, on a chief of the second a pale quarterly azure and gules. On the first and fourth a fleur-de-lys. In the second and third a lion passant quadrant all of the second, two roses gules seeded on barbed rest. Crest : a sphere without a frame bound with the zodiac in bend or, between two split pennons, flotant argent, each charged in chief with a cross gules. Over the sphere these words : " Deus indicat." Supporters : two sea lions or, the tails proper. Motto: " Deo ducente nil nocet."

It may be doubly interesting in these Chronicles to mention that in this year the East India Company dispatched three vessels to the Indies, viz. : " The Globe," " The Hector," and " The Thomas."

The " Globe " was intended for a trading voyage, but through the treachery of the Dutch she did not return till nearly four years afterwards. May it not fairly be assumed that the well-known '· Globe " Tavern adjoining to the yard, and apparently of about the same date was named after this long looked-for vessel ?

1614. In this year the East India Company dispatched the " New Year's Gift," of 650 tons, the " Hector," of 500 tons, the " Merchant's Hope," of 300 tons, and the " Solomon," of 200 tons. Some of these ships would not improbably have been built and fitted out in the Company's new 1615. dockyard at Blackwall. In the following year, however, the depressed state of the merchant shipping interest of England had again reached

*Lindsay's
History of
Merchant
Shipping.*
1616.

so low an ebb, that there were only ten ships belonging to the port of London of more than two hundred tons burthen. The work of fitting up the new East India Yard at Blackwall was evidently not yet quite completed, for the dockyard bell still bears the date of 1616, with a motto—" God be my good speed," together with two initials; and its weight: 3 cwt. 1 qr. 7 lbs. When weighed in 1865 it was found to weigh only 3 cwt. 0 qr. 27 lbs., having lost, according to this, 8 lbs. weight in two hundred and fifty years. The size of this bell is : height 1 ft. 6 in., breadth at top 1 ft. 1 in., at bottom 1 ft. 6 in.

1620.   On December 31st, 1620, the yard was leased by Nicholas Andrews to William Burrell for 464 years at a peppercorn rent. And on January 1621.   30th, 1621, William Burrell leased the same premises (reserving a certain right of way) to Sir Thomas Smith, Robert Johnson, Thomas Westrow and Jeffery Kirby for 463 years, from Lady-Day, 1620, at the rent of two shillings and sixpence payable at Michaelmas.

1629.   In the year 1629 there is mention of a great breach made in the South Marsh Wall (Isle of Dogs), when the whole level, it is stated, was exposed to danger.

It appears by extracts from the Court books of the Honourable 1632.   East India Company, that before the year 1632 the well-known Almshouses at Poplar, for invalided Petty Officers of the Company's ships had been 1637.   already founded. In the year 1637, King Charles II. added to the Royal Navy the largest vessel yet constructed, this was the " Sovereigne of the Seas," or " Royal Sovereign," a three-decked ship of nearly 150 guns designed and built at Woolwich Yard by Captain Phineas Pett, one of the principal officers of the Navy, shortly afterwards referred to as Sir Phineas Pett, and Mr. Peter Pett his son, who was the master builder, and had made the model of this ship before he was twenty-five years of age.   Of this young man a contemporary writer says : " Pallas herselfe flew into his bosome, and not only injoyned him to the undertaking, but inspired him in the manageing of so exquisite and absolute an architecture."   This famous ship is said to have been in length, by the keel, one hundred and twenty-eight feet ; in breadth, forty-eight feet ; in length, from the fore-end of the beak-head to the after-end of the stern, two hundred and thirty-two feet ; and in height, from the bottom of her keel to the top of her lanthorn, seventy-six feet ; she bore five lanthorns, the biggest of which would hold ten persons upright ; she had three flush-decks, a forecastle, half-deck, quarter-deck, and round-house.   Her lower tier had thirty ports ; middle tier, thirty ports ; third tier, twenty-six ports ; forecastle, twelve ports ; half deck, fourteen ports ; thirteen or fourteen ports more within board ; besides ten pieces of chace-ordnance forward ; ten right-aft ; and many loop-holes in the cabins for musket-shot. She had eleven anchors, one of four thousand four hundred pounds weight. She was of the burthen of one thousand six hundred and thirty-seven tons.

No further special record of the East India Yard is obtainable until we come to the time of Henry Johnson, whose name was for so many years pre-eminently associated with Blackwall. This Henry Johnson may have been connected with the Robert Johnson who leased the dockyard with Sir Thomas Smith, Thomas Westrow, and Jeffrey Kirby, in 1621, but of this we have no certain information. He was the eldest son of Francis Johnson, Esq., of Aldborough, in the county of Suffolk, and of Mary his wife, daughter of Peter Pett, of Deptford, in the county of Kent, brother of Sir Thomas Pett, knight.

1639. In the year 1639 Henry Johnson was apprenticed at the age of sixteen to his cousin Sir Phineas Pett, the well-known master shipbuilder, and it was probably upon the famous "Sovereigne of the Seas" already mentioned that young Henry Johnson learned his first lessons in the art of ship-building.

1642. In the year 1642 the inhabitants of Poplar and Blackwall renewed a request they had formerly made to the East India Company for a piece of ground to build a chapel on, and a house for the minister. It was then resolved by the Court that the ground behind the almshouses already spoken of should be granted for that purpose ; and that sixty loads of stones belonging to the Company, which lay there, should be given for the purpose of laying the foundation.

Chapter III.

1648. On December 13th, 1648, Henry Johnson, at the age of twenty-four, and having now completed his apprenticeship, married Dorothy, the daughter and heiress of William Lord, of Milton, in the County of Kent, Esq. ; at the time of her marriage, Dorothy Lord was only fifteen and a half years old. From Charnock's "Marine Architecture," we learn that in

1649. the following year, 1649, Henry Johnson, then of Deptford, where he doubtless had been led through the influence of his cousin, Sir Phineas Pett, launched the " Assurance " of 44 guns and 478 tons, and the " Assistance " of 42 guns and 555 tons.

The " Assurance " was at once commissioned and formed part of the fleet sent to reinforce Admiral Blake then cruising off Lisbon, his special object being to hunt down Prince Rupert, who, the Royal cause being now desperate on shore, was carrying on a guerilla, not to say piratical, warfare on his own account, and seizing any British ships he came across. This little known page of history is interesting, but to pursue it now would carry us too far from our subject. The " Assistance " took her full share in the action off Portland in 1653, when she was taken and retaken in the course of the day. Engagements such as these are doubtless represented in the panel paintings in the house in Blackwall Yard, where the Dutch flag is generally seen sinking to St. George's Cross. The " Assurance " is mentioned many years afterwards in a report on the Navy dated 1703, as " one of the old shipps built in the Parliament time."

It may be well to mention here the great difficulty which has naturally been experienced in obtaining reliable information as to the vessels built at this remote period. The records obtainable are most imperfect, and frequently for many years all records have been lost.

Returning now once more to Blackwall, we find by the Parliamentary survey in 1650, that the foundations of the East India Company's Chapel, for which a grant of land had been made in 1642, were by this time laid. The subscription for building this chapel was begun by Gilbert Dethick, Esq., with a benefaction of £100. The whole expense was above £2,000, and Sir Henry Johnson, whose arms were placed on the front of the gallery, was among the chief contributors. In 1652, upon another petition of the inhabitants, the East India Company voted the sum of £200 towards completing the work; and in the following year " the adventurers in the second general voyage, on a like petition, contributed another £50." The chapel was opened for service in 1654, when Thomas Walton was appointed chaplain by William Greenhill, vicar of Stepney.

In the year 1653, Charnock records that the " Dreadnought," of 62 guns and 732 tons, was built by Henry Johnson, of Blackwall; it is evident therefore that Henry Johnson must have migrated from Deptford to Blackwall since the year 1649. In 1654, the " York," of 62 guns and 749 tons, was built by Henry Johnson, and from an old record of some years later, we learn that " Many line of battle ships had been built in Blackwall Yard from

1650.

1652.

1653.

1654.

1654.

the year 1654." We may suppose therefore that the arrival of Henry Johnson at Blackwall had infused a fresh life into the building operations of the establishment.

1656. From parish records of this date we learn that Henry Johnson was interesting himself a good deal in the welfare and improvement of the neighbourhood. He was very active in the affairs of the hamlet, his name appearing in the minutes of nearly every meeting of the inhabitants from 1660. the year 1656, until the time of his death. In April, 1660, his name is mentioned as a member of the Commission of Sewers, formed in 1647, and 1661. he served the office of churchwarden in 1661. On January 15th, 1661, the celebrated Samuel Pepys, secretary to the Admiralty, makes the following note :—"We took barge and went to Blackwall, and viewed the Docke, [the Wet Dock], which is nearly made there, and a brave new merchantman, which is to be launcht shortly and they say to be called the ' Royal Oake.' Hence we walked to ' Dick Shoare,' [now called Duke Shore], and thence to the ' Toure,' and so home."

In April of this year, we find an account of another breach made in the Marsh wall (Isle of Dogs) which cost £16,000 to restore. This is probably the breach shown in Gascoyne's map, which was afterwards enlarged into the City Canal, and eventually became the South West India Dock in 1867.

1662. On January 16th, 1662, Evelyn relates in his Diary, that he "accompanied the Duke of York to an East India Vessel that lay at Blackwall, where we had entertainment of several curiosities. Amongst other spirituous drinks, as punch, &c., they gave us Canary that had been carried to and brought from the Indies, which was indeed incomparably good."

1665. On September 22nd, 1665, Samuel Pepys gives the following account of a second visit to Blackwall Yard. He says "At Blackwall there is observable what Johnson tells us, that in digging the late Docke, they did, twelve feet under ground find perfect trees overcovered with earth, nut trees, with the branches and the very nuts upon them; some of whose nuts he shewed us, their shells black with age, and their kernell, upon opening, decayed, but their shell perfectly hard as ever ; and a yew tree, (upon which the very ivy was taken up whole about it) which upon cutting with an addes, we found to be rather harder than the living tree usually is."

In this same year when the plague was at its height, Defoe paid a visit to the neighbourhood, which he describes in his " History of the Great Plague," and an extract from which we venture here to give at length.

" Much about the same time, I walked out into the fields towards Bow, for I had a great mind to see how things were managed in the river, and among the ships ; and as I had some concern in shipping, I had a notion that it had been one of the best ways of securing one's self from the infection to have retired into a ship, and musing how to satisfy my curiosity in that point, I turned away over the fields from Bow to Bromley and down to Blackwall, to the stairs that are there for landing or taking water.

" Here I saw a poor man walking on the bank or sea-wall as they call it, by himself, I walked awhile also about, seeing the houses all shut up ; at last I fell into some talk at a distance with this poor man. First, I asked how people did thereabouts ? Alas ! Sir, says he, almost desolate, all dead or sick : here are very few families in this part, or in that village, pointing at Poplar, where half of them are not dead already, and the rest sick. Then he, pointing to one house, they are all dead, said he, and the house stands open, nobody dares go into it. A poor thief, says he, ventured in to steal something, but he paid dear for his theft, for he was carried to the church-yard too last night. Then he pointed to several other houses. There, says he, they are all dead, the man and his wife and five children. There, says he, they are shut up, you see a watchman at the door, and so of other houses. Why, says I, what do you here all alone ? Why, says he, I am a poor desolate man, it hath pleased God I am not yet visited, though my family is, and one of my children dead. How do you mean then said I, that you are not visited ? Why, says he, that is my house, pointing to a very little low boarded house, and there my poor wife and two children live, said he, if they may be said to live, for my wife and one of the children are visited, but I do not come at them. And with that word I saw the tears run very plentifully down his face, and so they did down mine too, I assure you.

" But, said I, why do you not come at them ? How can you abandon your own flesh and blood ? Oh, sir, says he, the Lord forbid ; I do not abandon them, I work for them as much as I am able ; and, blessed be the Lord ! I keep them from want. And with that, I observed, he lifted up his eyes to Heaven with a countenance that presently told me I had happened on a man that was no hypocrite, but a serious, religious, good man ; and his ejaculation was an expression of thankfulness that, in such a condition as he was in, he should be able to say his family did not want. Well, says I, honest man, that is a great mercy as things go now with the poor. But how do you live, then, and how are you kept from the dreadful calamity that is now upon us all ? Why, sir, says he, I am a waterman, and there is my boat, says he, and the boat serves me for a house ; I work in it in the day, and I sleep in it in the night, and what I get, I lay it down upon that stone, says he, showing me a broad stone on the other side of the street, a good way from his house ; and then, says he, I halloa and call to them till I make them hear, and they come and fetch it.

"Well, friend, says I, but how can you get money as a waterman ? Does anybody go by water these times ? Yes, sir, says he, in the way I am employed there does. Do you see there, says he, five ships lie at anchor, pointing down the river a good way below the town ? and do you see, says he, eight or ten ships lie at the chain there, and at anchor yonder, pointing above the town. All those ships have families on board, of their merchants and owners and such like, who have locked themselves up, and live on board, close shut in for fear of the infection ; and I tend on them to fetch things for them, carry letters, and do what is absolutely necessary, that they may not be obliged to come on shore ; and every night I fasten my boat on board one of the ship's boats, and there I sleep by myself ; and, blessed be God, I am preserved hitherto.

"Well, said I, friend, but will they let you come on board after you have been on shore here, when this has been such a terrible place, and so infected as it is ?

"Why, as to that, said he, I very seldom go up the ship side, but deliver what I bring to their boat, or lie by the side, and they hoist it on board ; if I did, I think they are in no danger from me, for I never go into any house on shore, or touch anybody, no, not of my own family ; but I fetch provisions for them.

"Nay, says I, but that may be worse, for you must have those provisions of somebody or other ; and since all this part of the town is so infected, it is dangerous so much as to speak with anybody ; for the village, said I, is, as it were, the beginning of London, though it be at some distance from it.

"That is true, added he, but you do not understand me right. I do not buy provisions for them here ; I row up to Greenwich, and buy fresh meat there ; and sometimes I row down the river to Woolwich and buy there ; then I go to single farm houses on the Kentish side, where I am known, and buy fowls, and eggs, and butter, and bring to the ships, as they direct me, sometimes one, sometimes the other. I seldom come on shore here ; and I came only now to call my wife and hear how my little family do, and give them a little money which I received last night.

"Poor man! said I; and how much hast thou gotten for them?

"I have gotten four shillings, said he, which is a great sum, as things go now with poor men; but they have given me a bag of bread, too, and a salt fish, and some flesh; so all helps out.

"Well, said I, and have you given it them yet?

"No, said he, but I have called, and my wife has answered that she cannot come out yet, but in half-an-hour she hopes to come, and I am waiting for her. Poor woman! says he, she is brought sadly down; she has had a swelling, and it is broke, and I hope she will recover, but I fear the child will die; but it is the Lord! Here he stopt and wept very much.

"Well, honest friend, said I, thou hast a sure comforter, if thou hast brought thyself to be resigned to the will of God; He is dealing with us all in Judgment.

"Oh, sir, says he, it is infinite mercy if any of us are spared; and who am I to repine!

"Says't thou so, said I, and how much less is my faith than thine? And here my heart smote me, suggesting how much better this poor man's foundation was, on which he stayed in the danger than mine, that he had nowhere to fly, that he had a family to bind him to attendance which I had not, and mine was mere presumption, his a true dependence and a courage resting on God, and yet, that he used all possible caution for his safety.

"I turned a little away from the man, while these thoughts engaged me; for indeed, I could no more refrain from tears than he.

"At length, after some further talk, the poor woman opened the door, and called, Robert, Robert; he answered and bid her stay a few moments, and he would come; so he ran down the common stairs to his boat, and fetched up a sack in which was the provisions he had brought from the ships, and when he returned he hallooed again, then he went to the great stone which he showed me, and emptied the sack and laid all out everything by themselves, and then retired, and his wife came with a little boy to fetch them away; and he called and said: such a captain had sent such a thing, and such a captain such a thing, and at the end adds, God has sent it all, give thanks to Him. When the poor woman had taken up all, she was so weak she could not carry it at once in, though the weight was not much neither, so she left the biscuit which was in a little bag, and left a little boy to watch it till she came again.

"Well, but, says I to him, did you leave her the four shillings too, which you said was your week's pay?

" Yes, yes, says he, you shall hear her own it. So he calls again, Rachel, Rachel, which it seems was her name, did you take up the money? Yes, said she. How much was it? said he. Four shillings and a groat, said she. Well, well, says he, the Lord keep you all; and so he turned to go away.

" As I could not refrain from contributing tears to this man's story, so neither could I refrain my charity for his assistance, so I called him: Hark thee, friend, said I, come hither, for I believe thou art in health, that I may venture thee; so I pulled out my hand, which was in my pocket before. Here, says I, go and call thy Rachel once more, and give her a little more comfort from me; God will never forsake a family that trusts in Him, as thou dost; so I gave him four other shillings, and bid him go lay them on the stone, and call his wife.

" I have not words to express the poor man's thankfulness, neither could he express it himself, but by tears running down his face. He called his wife and told her God had moved the heart of a stranger, upon hearing their condition, to give them all that money, and a great deal more such as that he said to her. The woman too made signs of the like thankfulness, as well to Heaven as to me, and joyfully picked it up, and I parted with no money all that year that I thought better bestowed."

1666.

In the year 1666, the " Warspight," of 60 guns and 492 tons, was launched from Blackwall Yard. Concerning this vessel Pepys makes the following entry in his diary on May 19th. " Another great step and improvement to our navy, put in practice by Sir Anthony Deane, was effected in the ' Warspight ' and ' Defiance,' which were to carry six months' provisions, and their guns to be 4½ feet from the water."

On June 2nd, 1666, Pepys recounts the following incidents in connection with the embarkation of troops at Blackwall, in view of an expected attack from the Dutch fleet:—

" Up and to the office, where certain news is brought us of a letter come to the King this morning from the Duke of Albemarle, dated yesterday at eleven o'clock as they were sailing to the gun fleete, that they were in sight of the Dutch fleete, and were fitting themselves to fight them, so that they are ere this certainly engaged, besides, several do aver they heard the guns yesterday in the afternoon. This puts us at the Board into a tosse. Presently come orders for our sending away to the fleete a recruite of two hundred soldiers. So I rose from the table, and to the Victualler's Office, and thence upon the river among several vessels, to consider of sending them away and lastly down to Greenwich and there appointed two yachts to be ready for them, and did order the soldiers to march to Blackwall. Having set all things in order against the next flood, I went on shore with Captain Ewin at Greenwich, and into the Parke, and there we could hear the guns from the fleete most plainly. We walked to the waterside, and there seeing the King and Duke come down in their barge to Greenwich House, I to them, and did give them an account what I was doing. They went up to the Parke to hear the guns of the fleete go off. All our hopes now are that Prince Rupert, with his fleete, is coming back, and will be with the fleete this even, a message being sent to him to that purport on Wednesday last, and a return is come from him this morning that he did intend to sail from St. Ellen's point about four in the afternoon yesterday, which gives us great hopes, the wind being very fair, that he is with them this even, and the fresh going off of the guns makes us believe the same. Down to Blackwall, and there saw the soldiers (who were by this time gotten most of them drunk) shipped off. But Lord, to see how the poor fellows kissed their wives and sweethearts in that simple manner at their going off, and shouted, and let off their guns, was strange sport. In the evening come up the river the Katharine yacht, Captain Fazeby, who hath brought over my Lord of Alesbury (Robert Bruce, created earl of Alesbury 1663), and Sir Thomas Liddall (with a very pretty daughter, and in a pretty travelling dress) from Flanders, who saw the Dutch fleet on Thursday and ran from them, but from that hour to this hath not heard one gun, nor any news of any fight. Having put the soldiers on board, I home."

Sir Thomas Brame in a letter dated September 29th, 1666, writes that " Blackwall hath the largest wet docke in England, and belongs chiefly to the East India Company."

1667.

" On June 10th, the Dutch fleet, under Admiral de Ruyter, captured Sheerness and burnt several ships of the line, with the magazine containing stores valued at £40,000. The English, apprehensive that the enemy might venture up to London Bridge, sunk thirteen ships at Woolwich and four at Blackwall, and raised various platforms with artillery to defend the approaches to the City."

On June 14th, Pepys writes : "We do not hear that the Dutch are come to Gravesend, which is a wonder, but a wonderful thing it is that to this day we have not one word yet from Brouncker or Peter Pett or J. Minnes of anything at Chatham. At night come home Sir W. Batten and W. Pen, who only can tell me that they have placed guns at Woolwich and Deptford, and sunk some ships below Woolwich and Blackewall, and are in hopes that they will stop the enemy's coming up. But strange our confusion! that among them that are sunk, they have gone and sunk without consideration, "The Franclin," one of the King's ships, with stores to a very considerable value, that hath been long loaden for supply of the ships ; and the new ship at Bristoll and much wanted there, and nobody will own that they directed it, but do lay it on Sir W. Rider."

1677   Phineas Pett, in his journal, gives the following account of a visit which he paid to his nephew, Henry Johnson, at his seat at Friston, in company with Sir Anthony Deane, Surveyor to the Navy—

"Started, Tuesday, May 29th.

"On Tuesday, 5th of June, from Wickham we went to Friston to desire Mr. Johnson to go with us to Aldborough to view the ground and harbour and to see if a ship might be built there, which we found could be done ; then we returned and lay at Friston all night.

"Wednesday, 6th.—We departed from Friston and went to Yoxford, where Mr. Henry and Robert Cooper met us to treat about their timber ; Mr. Henry told us he had disposed of all his to Sir Henry Johnson, which would make about eighty load of 4-inch planks ; it was very good and large timber."

1678.   The year 1678 appears to have been a very important one in the life of Henry Johnson, for in this year he was elected with Sir Henry Haddock to represent his native town of Aldborough, in the Parliament, 1678–1679. In this year also he rebuilt the fine old red brick mansion which stands at the entrance of Blackwall Yard, and which bears on a tablet the inscription "Built 1612, Rebuilt 1678," with his own monogram between the dates. This excellent specimen of domestic architecture is worthy of remark. The principal rooms were panelled throughout with wainscot oak, richly carved after the fashion, if not by the hand of Grinling Gibbons and ornamented with the *panel paintings which have already been referred to. A large portrait of the "Royal Prince," built by Phineas Pett, at Woolwich, in 1610, adorned one mantel-piece, while a second was decorated with a portrait of the "Soveraigne of the Seas," launched from the same yard, 1637. These pictures had no doubt been placed here by Sir Henry Johnson in remembrance of his celebrated cousin, Phineas Pett, and of the ship on which he probably had learned his craft.

---

* These paintings are now in the possession of Robert Wigram, Esq.

1679.   In 1679, " The Essex," of 62 guns and 1072 tons and the " Kent," of 62 guns and 1069 tons, were built at Blackwall, and in this year Henry Johnson received in his own house the honour of knighthood from King Charles II. This distinction was no doubt well merited, and from a Sovereign who had paid such personal attention to the details of his navy, and was himself an inventor in matters connected with ship-building, it was a very natural token of sympathy and desire to foster and promote this national industry. The following extract from a letter, dated August 4th, 1673, which King Charles had written to Prince Rupert, shows the personal interest which he took in naval matters—" I am very glad the ' Charles ' does so well, a gerdeling this winter when she comes in will make her the best ship in England next summer. I believe if you try the two sloops that were built at Woolwich that have my invention in them, they will outsail any of the French sloops."

1680.   The sister ships, " Exeter" and " Suffolk," of 70 guns, were this year launched from Blackwall Yard.

1682.   On April 7th, 1682, a certain Samuel Moyer left by will to his son " one thirty-second part of a ship now building for Captain Dyk in Sir Henry Johnson's dock, for which £100 had been already paid." Also "one thirty-second part in each of the following ships in the service of the East India Company : the ' Defence,' Captain J. Heath, now on a voyage to the Bay of Bengal ; the 'Williamson,' Captain W. Busse, on a voyage to the Coast of Coromandel and Bay of Bengal ; and the ' Royal Resolution,' Captain Henry Wilshere, on a similar voyage." These ships had also probably been built in Sir Henry Johnson's yard.

1683.   Sir Henry Johnson died at the age of sixty, and was buried in the ground adjoining the East India Company's Chapel on Nov. 19th, 1683. He left two sons, Henry, the eldest, who succeeded him, and William, who is described in the records of Aldborough as a " capital burgess and once a bailiff," and who a few years later represented Aldborough in Parliament with his brother, and became ultimately Governor of Cape Coast Castle, where he died in 1718. By his will, dated September 14th, 1683, but proved only in 1688, Sir Henry Johnson, of Blackwall, knight, devised and bequeathed to his son Henry, afterwards Sir Henry Johnson, his heirs and assigns for ever, "all that his messuage or tenement wherein he then dwelt, situate and being at Blackwall aforesaid, and all other his messuages, yards, docks, cranes, wharfs, grounds, &c., with the appurtenances called the East India Yard, situate at or near Blackwall ; and all those three acres of land in the

South Marsh of Poplar, which he bought of Tweedie Crowder, upon trust to expend a sum of £300 for the building and erecting six good and substantial messuages or tenements upon the ground then called ‘ Globe Yard.’ Each house to contain two rooms, with a chimney in each room for the dwellinge and habitation of six poore aged shipp carpenters, either bachelors or widowers, every such shipp carpenter to be three score-years of age at least, each pensioner to receive two shillings and sixpence a week, and two shillings and sixpence extra on Christmas Eve, and a gowne of blue cloth of the value of thirty shillings, with his coat of arms in brass thereon, at least once a year.”

Strype in his edition of Stow’s “ Survey,” gives the following anecdote of Blackwall Yard at this period : “ In the time of the elder Sir Henry John-son, knight, ship-builder, an horse was wrought there thirty-four years, driven by one man, and he grew to that experience, that at the first sound of the bell for the men in the yard to leave off work, he also would cease labouring and could not by any means be brought to give one pull after it, and when the bell rang to work, he would as readily come forth again to his labour, which was to draw planks and pieces of timber from one part of the yard to another.” A public house in Blackwall, adjoining the yard, received the sign of the “ Old Hob,” in honour of the horse which bore that name, and which took this very independent mode of showing his importance.

The following description of the neighbourhood at this time, is from the same author : “ Of late years, Shipwrights and (for the most part) other Marine men have builded many large and strong houses for themselves, and smaller for saylors, from Radcliff almost to Poplar and so to Blackwall.” At Poplar that lyeth within the Parish of Stepney, is a Chapel and an Alms House for poor Seamen, both belonging to the old East India Company. Here is the Isle of Dogs, a fine rich level for fatning of cattle. Eight oxen fed here of late, were sold for £34 a-piece, and a hog fed here was sold for £20 and 6d. A butcher is said to have furnished a weekly club at Blackwall all the year round with a leg of mutton of 28lb. in weight, cut from a sheep in this marsh. Here is also a well-known wet Dock, called Blackwall Dock, belonging to Sir Henry Johnson, knight, very convenient for building and receiving of ships. About twenty years ago, more or less, in breaking up an old ship that was returned from the East Indies, they found a solid piece of oak in the keel, pierced eight inches deep, with a kind of horn that stuck fast in it. The master of the vessel did remember that when they were on the main sea the ship

C I

received a sudden shock which made it stop for the present, tho' it were in full sail At first they thought they had struck on a rock, but considering where they were they concluded that could not be, and they found no harm tho' they went down and searched the bottom of the ship, but they observed the sea bloody. But now the cause appeared that it was some sea fish that struck the ship, and broke his horn in the side of it."

It is probably to this horn that Evelyn refers in his diary, June 8th, 1664 : "To our Society to which his Majesty had sent that wonderful horn of the fish which struck a dangerous hole in the keel of a ship in the India Sea, which being broken off with the violence of the fish, and left in the timber, preserved it from foundering."

1685   Sir Henry Johnson was succeeded at Blackwall by his eldest son, Henry, who, two years after his father's death, was himself knighted in accordance with the custom of the time, which we believe almost invariably conferred this honour on the eldest sons of knights.

1688.   We find this year an apparently very accurate navy list, giving not only the names of all the Royal vessels, but also in most cases their place of building, and are thus able to identify as still afloat the " Dreadnought," "Exeter," " Essex," " Kent," "Suffolk," " Warspight," "York," "Assistance," and "Assurance," all built by Henry Johnson. This matter of identification is important and very difficult, as ships lost or destroyed were frequently replaced by others of the same name, and it is a matter of considerable difficulty to discriminate between the new and the old vessels.

1689.   The second Sir Henry Johnson, of Blackwall, was also made an Elder Brother of the Trinity House, and in 1689 was, with William Johnson, returned to Parliament for Aldborough, which place they represented together until the year 1714. He married Anne, daughter of Hugh Smithson, Esq., second son of Sir Hugh Smithson, of Stanwich, in the county of York, baronet. By this marriage he had one daughter, Anna, who was afterwards married to Thomas Wentworth, Earl of Strafford.

1690.   In 1690, the " Strombolo " fireship of 8 guns and 260 tons was launched, and in the month of October this year the " Dreadnought," 62 guns, built by the first Sir Henry Johnson in 1653, foundered off the North Foreland. A memorandum of this date referring to the state of the navy is interesting as having been written by Admiral Sir Cloudesley Shovell ; it suggests, among other things, "that the masts of the ' Kent ' (built at Blackwall, 1679) should be shortened two feet, and the tops widened eight inches on a side, and to be made oval." The " Warspight," " Essex,"

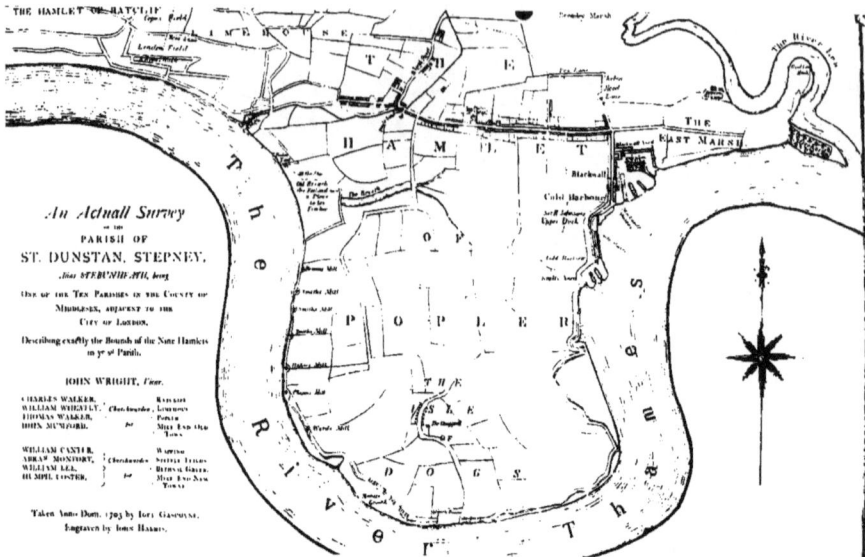

THE HAMLET OF RATCLIF

An Actuall Survey
OF THE
PARISH OF
ST. DUNSTAN, STEPNEY,
alias STEBUNHEATH, being

ONE OF THE TEN PARISHES IN THE COUNTY OF
MIDDLESEX, ADJACENT TO THE
CITY OF LONDON.

Describing exactly the Bounds of the Nine Hamlets
in ye sd Parish.

JOHN WRIGHT, *Chur.*

CHARLES WALKER,   RATCLIFF
WILLIAM WHITELY,   *Churchwardens* LIMEHOUSE
THOMAS WALKER,   POPLAR
JOHN MUMFORD,   *for*   MILE END OLD
                         TOWN

WILLIAM CARTER,   WAPPING
ABRAM MONFORT,   *Churchwardens* SPITTLE FIELDS
WILLIAM LEE,   )   BETHNAL GREEN
HUMPH. LOSTER,   )   *for*   MILE END NEW
                         TOWN

Taken Anno Dom. 1703 by JOS: GASCOINE.
Engraved by JOHN HARRIS.

"Suffolk," "Exeter," and "York" were all engaged this year against the Dutch in the action off Beachy Head.

1691.

In September, 1691, the "Exeter," of 70 guns, built by Sir Henry Johnson's father, was blown up at Plymouth. An interesting relic of this date was found in Blackwall Yard during the alterations made by the Midland Railway Company in 1878. This was a brass two-foot rule, similar to the rules now used by shipwrights, with name and date—"Edward Gast, 1691."

1694.
1695.

In 1694 the "Blaze" fireship, of 8 guns, was built at Blackwall, and in the following year the "Burlington," of fifty guns. On the 25th of November of this year eleven acres of copyhold land at Blackwall were surrendered to Sir Henry Johnson by Henry Dethick, Esq., one of an old and influential family, whose name is frequently mentioned in the records of this hamlet. The portrait of Sir Gilbert Dethick, Garter Principal King of Arms, still hangs in the hall of the College of Arms.

1703.

In 1703 Sir Henry Johnson married for his second wife Martha, only daughter and heiress of John Lord Lovelace, of Hurley, in the county of Berks, declared Baroness Wentworth, and so walked at the coronation of Queen Anne, 1702. She died a widow without issue in 1745, at the age of about eighty-five years.

1704.

In this year was gained the important naval victory off Malaga, the Trafalgar, as it has been called, of the 18th century; this was a great day for the Blackwall ships present under the orders of Admirals Sir George Rooke and Sir Cloudesley Shovell, the "Essex," "Kent," the "Old Assurance," and the "Warspight," which last suffered very severely. No such victory had been gained over the Spanish flag since the Armada ; indeed, with Malaga and the capture of Gibraltar at sea, and Blenheim on land, this year must unquestionably stand one of the foremost in the annals of England.

1705.

1706

Returning once more to Blackwall we learn from Stow that in the year 1705 "were two whales of different sorts brought and cut up at Blackwall, and in this year a 50-gun frigate, called the 'Blackwall,' was captured by the French." For the following remarkable anecdote we are again indebted to Stow : "A person lately living in this hamlet [Poplar and Blackwall] having a great concern for the safety of a ship that was like to break her back at Blackwall, had his blood and spirits set into such an extraordinary ferment, or ebullition rather, by the fear of her miscarriage, that by the violence of it the tops of the nails of his hands and feet were cast off to a great distance from their natural situation, and so remained to his death, and many persons now living have attested the same."

The "Deal Castle," of 24 guns, was captured by the French this year, and the "Squirrel," of 24 guns, foundered off the coast of Holland. Both these ships had been built in Blackwall Yard.

1707. The "Kent" captured the new French frigate "Superbe," of 56 guns; and the "Suffolk" took the French frigate "Guillard," of 56 guns. Among a number of old plans of ships of war belonging to this period, and which are carefully preserved in the archives of the Yard, there is a very perfect drawing of the "Suffolk," 70 guns; unfortunately, however, many of these plans have neither name nor date, and consequently cannot be identified.

The "Essex," "Kent," "Warspight," "Squirrel," and other vessels built in Blackwall Yard, are repeatedly mentioned about this time as serving in the fleets under the commands of Admirals Sir George Rooke, Sir Cloudesley Shovell, and Sir George Byng.

1708. About this time the manager of Sir Henry Johnson's Yard was a certain Philip Perry, whose history and introduction to Blackwall has been given as follows. In or about the year 1690, Philip Perry was a carpenter on board of one of His Majesty's ships. During a severe storm the vessel was in much danger of foundering from a bad leak, but in consequence of Philip Perry's skill and ingenuity the ship was saved and brought safely back to port. The Commissioners of the Admiralty, to mark their appreciation of his service, gave him an important post at Plymouth Dockyard, whence he was transferred to Deptford, where he greatly increased his reputation. This position he is said to have relinquished to superintend Sir Henry Johnson's business at Blackwall.

1709. The "Assurance" and "Assistance," with three other vessels, engaged in a bloody conflict with four French frigates; the battle was fought in the Channel, and victory to the last remained doubtful, neither side making a capture, while much about the same time the "Kent" brought two prizes into Plymouth.

In this year too the "Suffolk" and "Kent" formed part of the fleet which, under Admiral Byng, attempted the relief of Alicante. The story of this siege is so remarkable an instance of English dogged courage, and is besides so little known, that we shall make no apology for giving it at length.

"The garrison, driven by the besiegers into the almost impregnable citadel which from the top of a lofty crag overhangs the town, awaited there the formation and firing of the mine which was to blow the whole fortress into the air. Due notice of the event was given by the chivalrous Spanish commander, who himself escorted a deputation of the besieged over his work, and earnestly hoped they would do him the honour of surrendering before 6. A.M. of the third day. All to no purpose. Major-Gen. Richards, while fully recognizing the skill with which the mine was laid, regretted his inability to meet the Don's wishes, and at 5.30 A.M. repaired to the west battery, where he could see the fuse ignited. He had not long to wait, punctual to time himself with his field officers, their company, ten guns, and about eighty sentinels, women and peasants, were blown into the air; but thanks to a counter-mine, enough of the castle yet remained to enable Lieut.-Col. D'Albon to hold out until the arrival of the fleet, on board which he, with the remnants of his garrison, safely embarked."

> " Time preserves the Spartan story of Leonidas's glory,
> How with his brave three hundred Persia's swarms he held at bay ;
> Fame records the Switzer's daring, who Burgundian overbearing,
> Tamed hundreds matched 'gainst thousands on Morgarten's bloody day ;
> But Swiss nor Spartan annals contain no deed more glorious,
> No feat of stubborn hardihood o'er mightier odds victorious."

1710.
The fleet cruising off the Lizard sighted the French squadron, when the " Kent," " York " and " Assurance " were immediately ordered to give chase ; these vessels were apparently good sailors, for both the " Kent " and " Assurance " made prizes, after a severe action, for which Captain Johnson obtained great credit ; it must, however, be admitted, that he had a real superiority in guns. In this year, too, the " Warspight " aided in taking the French frigate, the " Moor," and this is the last performance of our

1713.
vessels before the Treaty of Utrecht, in 1713, put for a time an end to their adventures.

1714.
In an account of the stopping of the great breach at Dagenham this year by Captain John Perry, the well-known civil engineer, who is supposed to have been the eldest brother of the Philip Perry before-mentioned, reference is made to a pontoon built expressly to assist in closing the breach ; the first attempt at closing did not, however, prove successful, and the " aforesaid machine," as it is called, " which was built at Blackwall, rose up from the ground and broke and tore to pieces."

1718.
Peace in these days was seldom of long continuance, and in this year we have again to record one of the great naval victories of the 18th century. Admiral Byng encountered the Spanish fleet off Cape Passaro, and defeated them with the loss of some fifteen Spanish vessels ; the " Essex " was

engaged, and so of course was the "Kent," who, with her quondam enemy the "Superbe," especially distinguished themselves, capturing between them the Spanish Admiral's vessel. The Spaniards taken they allege at a disadvantage, for war had hardly been declared, offered no very formidable resistance, "their ships," says the chronicler, "being old, their artillery none of the best, and their seamen not to be depended on."

1719.

On May 19th, 1718, Sir Henry Johnson, being in a declining state of health, devised his Blackwall property to William Guidot, Thomas Tooke and George Tooke, their heirs and assigns upon trust for sale, for payment of his debts, legacies, and funeral expenses, and on September 24th, 1719, he died at Bath, and was buried at Tuddington. Administration was granted to Thomas, Earl of Strafford, the husband of his only child, Anna, during the minority of their two daughters, Anna and Lucy Wentworth.

Many years later Sir Henry Johnson's representative, Agneta Johnson, daughter of Henry Johnson, Esquire, of Berkhampstead, described as a great heiress, married in 1769 the Honourable Charles Yorke, brother of Lord Chancellor Hardwicke. Portraits of this lady and of Sir Phineas Pett are now at Wimpole, in Lord Hardwicke's possession.

1723.

In the unfortunate expedition to the West Indies, under Admiral Hosier, we are not able to trace any record of our Blackwall ships, and when the ghost of that ill-fated commander complained so pathetically—

> "I with thirty sail attended, did the Spanish town affright,
> Nothing then their wealth defended, but my orders not to fight,"

it is satisfactory to think that not one of the thirty was the workmanship of either Henry Johnson or Philip Perry.

1724.

On June 17th, Thomas Wentworth, Earl of Strafford, and Anna, his countess, with the concurrence of William Guidot and George Tooke, the surviving trustees of Sir Henry Johnson's will, sold and conveyed to Captain John Kirby, on behalf of himself and his partners, Captains E. Pierson, Jonathan Collett, and Richard Boulton, for the sum of £2,800, all that capital messuage or mansion house at Blackwall, with garden terrace walk on east side of same, and the orchard on north side of the yard, three acres.

All that yard called East India Yard.

Also a wet dock, 3 dry docks, and 4 launches in yard, storehouses on north and east sides of yard, 3 messuages or tenements and smith's shop in said yard, in occupation of Robert Wynne, Edward Hall, and John Crowley, Esquires.

Sir Henry Johnson, eldest son, bapt. at Aldborough, afsd. 25 Jan., 1623, of Blackwall, in the County of Middlesex, and of Friston Hall, in the County of Suffolk. Apprentice to his Cousin, Sir Phineas Pett, 1639; Knighted in his own house by King Charles II., 1679; Member of Parliament for Aldborough: died 1683, buried at Poplar 19 Nov., 1683; Will proved 1688.

1st Wife.

Anne, daur. of Hugh Smithson, Esquire, second son of Sir Hugh Smithson, of Stanwick, in the County of York, Baronet.

Dorothy, daur. and heir of William Lord, of Milton, in the County of Kent, Esq., by Margaret his wife, daughter and heir of .... Mason: married 13 December, 1648, she then aged 15½, and he 24 years: she died 5 Nov., 1664.

Henry Johnson, Esquire, eldest son, Knighted in 1685, an Elder Brother of the Trinity House and Representative in Parliament for Aldborough, in the County of Suffolk: died 29 Sept., 1719, buried at Teddington.

Francis Johnson, 2d son, bapt. at Aldborough 24 Feb., 1627, ancestor of Bertezwick Johnson, Esq., many years in the Commission of the Peace for Middlesex, who left two daughters, his co-heirs.

2d Wife.

Martha, only daur. and heir of John Lord Lovelace, of Hurley, in the County of Berks, declared Baroness Wentworth, and so walked at the Coronation of Queen Anne, 1702: died without issue, 1745, having never had any child.

Elizabeth, married to Captain Parish, of the Navy, buried in the family vault at Poplar.

Coach houses and stables in said yard, and other buildings belonging to mansion and yard, 17 messuages in a row on south side of mansion.

Messuage on north side of mansion house by the sign of the "Globe," with Globe yard and appurtenances, slaughter house and 9 messuages in a row adjoining eastward to the same, 7 of which were used as almshouses, which capital messuage, and the 17 houses, and the "Globe" contained in front westward to Poplar Marsh, from north to south 584 feet. Also causeway leading from east end of Poplar town southwards towards the Thames, in length from north to south on the west side 1,122 feet, and on the east side 1,076 feet, in breadth from east to west 26 feet, and the toll of said causeway, and ropewalk, in length 1,122 and width 28 feet, and smith's shop at north end of causeway, in possession of John Harding.

Also the warehouse at south end of ropewalk.

And three fields or closes of marsh land lying on the east side of mansion, late in occupation of John Kirby, or his assigns, 8 acres, and the forelanes to the same belonging.

Coach houses and stables in yard, and 3 acres of marsh land on south Poplar Marsh.

All which premises are situate at Blackwall, together with other premises, and contained in the whole 20½ acres.

And all other hereditaments and premises of said Earl and Countess and said W. Guidot and George Tooke, and late of Sir Henry Johnson, situate in the hamlets of Poplar and Blackwall aforesaid (except copyholds which were intended to be surrendered).

This purchase was made subject to the first Sir Henry Johnson's bequest for building almshouses, which up to this time had not been properly carried into effect.

The houses had been partially built, but appropriated to other uses, and the benefits of the bequest withheld under the pretence of a want of proper objects as described by the donor's will. In this year, however, the inhabitants of the hamlet took the matter up, and the Earl of Strafford then consented to allow the sum of £300 out of the purchase money for building other houses, without further litigation, the inhabitants remitting the arrears, which they were induced the rather to do as Sir Henry Johnson the younger, though he had neglected to pay the pensions, had provided several poor carpenters with habitations rent free, and his ship yard had been of great service to the hamlet.

1726.

The "Kent" put a pleasing finale to the performances of this war by carrying Admiral Wagers' flag to the relief of Gibraltar, into which place he was able to throw much needed succour and provisions.

The peace which again followed in the succeeding year, leaves us for a time with nothing to record of the Blackwall frigates, and although this did not last very long, we are bound to admit that the next thirty years are not among the brightest in our naval annals; little appears to have been attempted and less done, and although various successes against the Spaniards in the East Indies are an exception to the prevailing dulness, it is not until the elder Pitt's accession to power in 1757 that anything like life appears to have been reinfused into our navy.

1728.

In this year the Rev. Gloster Ridley (so called from having been born on board the "Gloucester" East Indiaman), minister of Poplar Chapel, and others, applied to the then proprietors of Blackwall Yard, Captain Collett and Captain Boulton, to have the six carpenters put into the alms-houses as arranged. The reply received was, that if six properly qualified persons could be found they should be put in.

Chapter III.

After the sale of the Blackwall Yard Estate by the Earl and Countess of Strafford, Philip Perry, who had for some years been managing the business for Sir Henry Johnson, took a lease of the premises, and with his son John continued the business on his own account under the style of P. Perry and Co. This firm is frequently referred to in "Charnock's Marine Architecture," as constructing vessels for the navy. Philip Perry

1732.

died on the 26th of September, 1732, at the age of sixty-one years, and was buried near the first Sir Henry Johnson, in the ground adjoining the East India Company's, or Poplar, Chapel, as it was now called. After his death the business was carried on by his son, who, as we learn from local records, had become by this time a person of considerable influence in the neighbourhood.

1736.

A very perfect drawing still remains in the Yard of the "Weymouth," 60 guns, launched 31st March, 1736, with a memorandum stating that she was lost on Sandy Island at Antigua, 15th February, 1744.

1739.

Mr. Perry's eldest son Philip was born at Blackwall in this year.

ALMOUTH Capt. Thos FIELD Launch'd at BLACKWALL the 24 of August 1752 Length ? Keel 100½, Breadth 35, Burthen 811

1741.   In the year 1741, the " Leopard," of 50 guns and 872 tons, was launched, and the ever active " Kent," under Captain Fox, is again heard of at the conquest of Cuba, intercepting a San Domingo convoy, valued at nearly a million sterling.

1742.   In 1742, we find from an old list of docks, that Perry's Yard at this time " had a wet dock, three dry docks, one double and two single, as well as building slips for many ships of war."

1743.   Mr. Perry's second son, John, who afterwards became so widely known in connection with Blackwall Yard, at the time when it was spoken of as " more capacious than any other private dockyard in the kingdom, or probably in the world," and also as the constructor and sole owner of the Brunswick Basin and the adjoining Mast House, was born this year.

1745.   In 1745, we have accounts of the " Norwich," 48 guns and 993 tons, being rebuilt at Blackwall Yard.

1747.   An old plan of this date speaks of the East India Company as still occupying part of the yard, Captain Collett being the proprietor. The drawings of a ship of 366 tons built in this year are also preserved in the office. The " Kent " again takes a share in Admiral Hawke's engagement off Cape Finisterre, but here for the first time in her long and adventurous career the gallant " Kent " earns no laurel. A court-martial was called on Captain Fox at the request of the Admiral, " for not doing his utmost to engage, distress, and damage the enemy." Though acquitted of the capital charge of cowardice, he was dismissed his vessel in that he had paid too much attention to the advice of his first lieutenant and master. " Two —— bad fellows," adds Keppel, who himself sat on the court-martial, " who, I verily believe, did their best to ruin him."

1750.
1752.   The " Falmouth," East Indiaman, was commenced by Mr. Perry on the 22nd of August, 1750, and launched on the 14th of August, 1752, a copy of one of the elaborate plans of this vessel now hanging in the office at Blackwall is here given. In this year Mr. Perry's wife, Ann Perry, died at the age of thirty-six.

1755.   Until the year, 1755, Sir Henry Johnson's charitable bequest had remained uncompleted, but now, after some litigation, a compromise took place, and Keble Gray, a parishioner, bachelor, and ship carpenter, 60 years of age; George Trewitt, ditto, widower, 64; William Wentworth, Limehouse, ditto, 79 ; John How, ditto, 77 ; John Jackson, of Rotherhithe, widower, 63 ; and Thomas Rising, of Woolwich, bachelor, 62, were admitted.

The pensions were after this regularly paid by the proprietors of

Blackwall Yard ; but instead of the "goune of blue cloth" the inhabitants received the value in the necessaries of life every Christmas. The houses have since then been rebuilt.

1756.   The "Deal Castle," of 20 guns and 407 tons, was launched by John Perry and Co. She was at once commissioned, and made her first cruise under Howe, aiding in the relief of the Channel Islands then threatened by the French.

1757.   The "Osterley," East Indiaman, 642 tons, Captain Vincent, was launched September 29th, 1757 ; this vessel was afterwards captured by the French, but again recaptured some years later. The "Tilbury," East Indiaman, 642 tons, Captain Mainwaring, was launched October 14th.

1758.   The "Valentine," East Indiaman, 655 tons, Captain Fernall, was launched September 19th, 1758, and the "Ajax," East Indiaman, 655 tons, Captain Lindsay, on December 16th.

The "Essex" this year conveyed the Duke of Marlborough, together with a considerable body of men, to the coast of France. The troops were landed without difficulty, but very little else was attempted, and the expedition returned in one month from starting, having proved, says Walpole, that it is not every Duke of Marlborough who can conquer the French. Prior to this date, but after 1748, the old "Assurance," the patriarch of the fleet, had been condemned to be broken up, having outlived by many years both the Johnsons and Philip Perry.

1759.   In 1759 the "Essex" and "Warspright," lately rebuilt, took part in Admiral Hawke's dashing action with the French off Belleisle. The weather was tremendous, so much so that one French vessel went down through the water she took in at her lower deck ports, and the wind was dead on shore ; but tough old Admiral Hawke was still more tremendous, and on this shore he succeeded in driving several of the enemy, but unfortunately the "Essex," together with the "Resolution," shared the same fate.

At Blackwall Yard, the "Duke of Richmond," East Indiaman, 656 tons, Captain Godfrey, was launched on September 8th, 1759; the "Norfolk," 662 tons, Captain Bonham, on October 2nd ; and the "Neptune," 656 tons Captain Purling, on December 6th. The "Firm," of 60 guns and 1,297 tons, was also launched this year for the government.

1761.   The "Earl of Elgin," East Indiaman, 687 tons, Captain Evans, was launched January 22nd, 1761, and the "Royal Charlotte," 669 tons, Captain Clements, on October 29th. The "Africa," of 64 guns and 1,354 tons, was also launched for the government.

1762.   The "Clive," East Indiaman, 687 tons, Captain Allen, was launched January 26th, 1762.

This year, when Spain joined in the war, became one of unusual pressure upon the resources of the country, many towns and even individuals, joined in contributing vessels ; and if, as has been stated, the firm at Blackwall ever took this course, it is not impossible that it may have been at this date.

1763.   The "Earl of Middlesex," East Indiaman, of 670 tons, Captain Fletcher was launched February 2nd, 1763; the "Bute," of 670 tons, Captain Maitland, on February 3rd ; the "Talbot," 670 tons, Captain Dethick, on February 14th; the "Anson," 670 tons, Captain Chick, on October 24th ; and the "Devonshire," of 670 tons, Captain Quick, on November 7th.

1764.   The "Asia," of 670 tons, Captain English, was launched on January 4th, 1764 ; the "Salisbury," of 670 tons, Captain Bromfield, on October 11th ; and the "Thames," of 692 tons, Captain Harris, on October 24th. The "St. Albans," of 64 guns and 1,380 tons, was also launched for the government.

1765.   The "Harcourt," East Indiaman, of 688 tons, Captain Rodham, was launched January 22nd, 1765 ; the "Duke of Cumberland," of 729 tons, Captain Glover, on August 2nd ; the "Prince of Wales," 729 tons, Captain Court, on September 16th; the "Duke of Kingston," 687 tons, Captain Morrison, on October 16th ; and the "Hampshire," 709 tons, Captain Smith, on October 31st.

1766.   The "Hector," of 702 tons, Captain Williams, was launched September 5th, 1766 ; the "Europa," of 692 tons, Captain Pelly, on October 6th ; and the "Earl of Chatham," 692 tons, Captain Morris, on December 17th.

1767.   The "Valentine," of 692 tons, Captain Ogilvie, was launched September 25th, 1767 ; the "Verelst," 692 tons, Captain Baddison, on October 9th ; and the "Shrewsbury," 692 tons, Captain Jones, on November 23rd.

1768.   Mr. Robert Wigram, who was afterwards well known in connection with Blackwall, sailed as surgeon on board the "Duke of Richmond," bound for St. Helena.

1770.   The same Robert Wigram was in this year surgeon on board the "British King," bound for St. Helena, Bancoolen and China.

1771.   Chamberlain's History and Survey of London gives the following description of the neighbourhood at this time :—

" The hamlet of Poplar and Blackwall, which forms a street upwards of a mile in length, is inhabited by seafaring people, and such as are concerned in ship-building. About the middle of Poplar, on the north side, is a set of almshouses founded for the widows of seamen in the India service, adjoining to which is a large chapel of ease to this part of the parish of St. Dunstan, Stepney."

" Blackwall is remarkable for the mooring of Indiamen at the stairs, and for a considerable ship yard where many East Indiamen are both laid up and built."

1772.　　Mr. Perry died at Blackwall, and was buried with his wife and father in the grounds of Poplar chapel. His grandson, Mr. Richard Perry, writes of this:—" My grandfather was of a very religious turn, and was supposed by the family to have passed away while engaged in his devotions ('Beatus ille!'). He had retired to his chamber one evening for that purpose, and was found dead upon the floor; the candle had fallen from his hand, and had providentially become extinguished." Mr. Perry left two sons and several daughters. His eldest son Philip died shortly afterwards, and his second son John succeeded him in business. By his will, dated 1772, " Mr. John Perry, of Blackwall, shipbuilder, left the interest of £200 to be given half-yearly in bread to the poor of the hamlet."

1774.　　The " Jamaica," West Indiaman, Captain Crossman, was launched August 25th, 1774.

1775.　　In this year the contract for building the " Hornet" sloop, of 14 guns and 300 tons, was signed.

1776.　　The " Vesuvius" bomb vessel of 298 tons, the "Ariel" of 20 guns and 429 tons, and the " Aurora" 28 guns and 583 tons, were contracted for. In this year Philip Perry, eldest son of the late Mr. Perry, died at the age of thirty-seven, and his brother John became the head of the firm. This John Perry was a very remarkable man; he had been educated at Harrow, where he had formed a friendship with the afterwards celebrated linguist Sir William Jones; he was a strong politician, and a strenuous supporter of Mr. Pitt, he possessed great natural ability and remarkable perseverance. We shall refer however more particularly to his works later on.

1777.　　The " Aurora," 28 guns, was launched June 7th, 1777, and the "Ariel," 20 guns, on July 7th; also "in the seventeenth year of King George III," as the contract expresses it, the " Southampton," East Indiaman, of 758 tons, was contracted for with Mr. Charles Foulis, of Woodford.

1778　　War having now been declared, it will easily be understood that for this and the next few years the yard was full of building and repairing work for the Government. The "Belliqueux," 64 guns and 1376 tons, and the "Bonetta," 14 guns and 300 tons, were contracted for; and the "Hornet," 14 guns, was launched. A memorandum of Mr. Perry's at this date has reference to the launching of the "Atlas," which vessel appears to have stuck on the ways, and been with difficulty got off. Mr. Perry attributes this mishap to the grease not having been boiled. Another accident also occurred this year from the bursting in of the double dock gates, the rush of water being so great as to carry the wing transom of an East Indiaman from the stern of the dock to a considerable distance.

Three merchant ships were also contracted for with Sir Charles Raymond, of Valentines, Essex, in place of the "Duke of Richmond," "Clive," and "Havannah." It may here be mentioned that the East India Company were in the habit of chartering vessels practically for a lifetime, and when such vessels were either worn out, lost, or otherwise rendered unserviceable, their privileges with the Company were transferred to other vessels built to take their places.

1779   This year another ship of war was launched, and the "Devonshire" and "Thames" were contracted for with Mr. Foulis "on the same terms as the three vessels built last year for Sir Charles Raymond." The "London," East Indiaman, of 753 tons, was contracted for with Mr. Webb on the same terms as the previous vessel, and the "Harcourt" was contracted for with Thomas Newt, Esq.; the tonnage is not always mentioned in these cases, but the dimensions do not vary much, being generally about 116 feet in length and 36 feet in breadth, that is about 3⅓ breadths to length. The "Crown," of 64 guns and 1387 tons, was also contracted for on the same terms as the "Belliqueux."

On September 7th, Mr. Perry purchased the whole of the Blackwall Yard estate from Henry Boulton, together with other property in Poplar, for the sum of £8,000, "subject as to the three acres of copyhold enfranchised to the Charity under Sir Henry Johnson's will."

1780.   The "Colebrook" was contracted to be built for J. Boulton, Esq., and verbally Charles Foulis contracted for another vessel to replace the "Thames." We have also records in this year of some heavy repairs being effected to the "Maidstone," 28 guns, and to the "Boston," 32 guns.

1781.   "The "Busbridge," East Indiaman, of 771 tons, was contracted for with Robert Preston, Esq., and in this year was signed the contract for building the "Venerable," "Victorious," "Hannibal," and "Theseus." of

74 guns and 1652 tons, vessels which became well known in the naval history of this stirring period, but before their fighting days began they had in common with the other vessels building at the time obtained a very noteworthy position in the financial records of the Yard. The declaration of peace in the early part of 1783, before these contracts were completed, caused no doubt a great and immediate fail in the cost of all materials and labour ; the Government was in no hurry to take possession of their new vessels, and consequently the profits on this and similar transactions at the time were very large.

1782.

In the year 1782, George Green, of whom we shall say more presently, came to Blackwall yard at the age of 15, and was apprenticed to his future father-in-law, Mr. John Perry. The "Gorgon" and "Adventure," of 44 guns, were contracted for, and in this year Mr. Perry constructed a small dock, just large enough to receive one whaling vessel ; this little dock was many years afterwards altered into a building slip.

1783.

In an old memorandum book of this date we find the following entry:— "J. Perry & Co. send to six different officers of Woolwich Dockyard two dozen of port and one dozen of Madeira," with the following delicate note : "J. Perry & Co.'s comps. to————and having taken the liberty to send some wine as an acknowledgment for the trouble which they in the course of their engagements subject him to, hope he will excuse the indelicacy of their desiring to know whether it came safe." The "Victorious," 74 guns, was launched this year, Mr. Edward Hunt being surveyor to the navy. The close of the war had naturally put an end for the time to all further contracts with the Government for new ships, and a memorandum book of this date from which many of these particulars have been taken, has for the next few years no further entries of such contracts.

1784.

The year 1784, which has been frequently referred to in connection with the number of large ships building at this time, is described as having been a very important one in the history of the firm, the tide of business was at the full, and Mr. Perry is said to have been almost alarmed at his own success. There was a full revival of trade and prosperity after the accomplishment of American independence, which had been expected to ruin English trade entirely.

Mr. Perry Watlington, of Moor Hall, Harlow, the present seat of the Perry family, has in his possession a picture of Blackwall Yard taken about this time. Seven ships are shown upon the stocks, the "Venerable," "Victorious," "Hannibal," and "Theseus," seventy-fours, the "Gorgon" and

BLACKWALL.

This view was taken at the Launch of the "BOMBAY CASTLE," a 74 Gun Ship, built at the expense of the Honble. East India Company, and presented by them to His Majesty.

Blackwall is the most eminent place on the River Thames for building and equipping Ships for the service of the Honble. East India Company... ...the East India Dock ...and ... ...the Battle Ship... ...and many have ...with the finest of Stores ...for Ships of war... ...were upon the occasion that ... ...

Published March 3th ... PUBLISHED N ... C. ... &c.1

"Adventure," forty-fours, and the West Indiaman, "Three Sisters;" the "Busbridge" has just been launched, and four other vessels are in dry dock under repair; a similar picture is also in the possession of Messrs. Money Wigram and Sons.

1785.
1786.
In the year 1785 was launched the "Venerable," 74 guns, Lord Duncan's future flag ship at the battle of Camperdown, and in the following year, her not less famous sister vessels "Hannibal" and "Theseus" were launched, Sir Thomas Slade being surveyor to the navy.

1788.
The West Indiaman, "Three Sisters," was launched.

1789.
The "Bombay Castle," of 74 guns, and 1,612 tons, was launched. This splendid ship had been built at the sole expense of the Honourable East India Company, and by them presented to His Majesty King George III. A copy of the interesting print representing the launch of this vessel is here given. So magnificent and patriotic a gift significantly shows the noble liberality which has rendered the Honourable India East Company for all time a type of the true merchant princes. The "Bombay Castle" was subsequently engaged in the attack on the Cape of Good Hope.

In 1789 we first hear of a commercial dock in connection with Blackwall yard, and the cause of its being undertaken was as follows :—

Ever since the time of the great fire in 1666 the port of London had remained entirely unchanged in respect of dock accommodation. The merchants complained loudly of the great inconvenience which they were forced to endure, and under these circumstances Mr. Perry determined to construct a dock himself. With the help of Mr. Pouncey, the engineer whom he employed, he commenced on the 2nd of March, 1789, at his own expense, the construction of a basin, on the north-east boundary of his yard, intended chiefly for the accommodation and protection of the ships of the Honourable East India Company. This basin, which in honour of King George he named the Brunswick basin, though by nearly everybody else it was called "Perry's Dock," has an area of about eight acres, and was divided into two parts, each part having its own entrance; the one part was intended to receive about thirty of the largest East India ships, and the other an equal number of smaller vessels. At the west end stood the well-known Mast House, a building 120 feet high, which, in addition to its original purpose for lifting the masts in and out of vessels and stowing the sails and rigging of East Indiamen, served for many years as a conspicuous landmark, regarded with varying interest by the numerous outward and homeward-bound vessels which passed continually up and down the river.

E

The first ship masted here on the 25th October, 1791, was the " Lord Macartney," East Indiaman. The whole suit of masts and bowsprit were raised and fixed in 3 hours 40 minutes.

This mast house was taken down by the East and West India Dock Company in 1862.

The Southern quay, which was eleven hundred feet in length, was supplied with cranes for landing guns and heavy stores, and the East quay had conveniences for receiving blubber from the whale ships, and warehouses for storing whalebone.

At the time of its construction, this dock, which belonged entirely to Mr. Perry, was the only dock of its kind in London, though there were several at the out ports. Its construction occupied two years, which were to Mr. Perry two years of the deepest anxiety and toil; the work was successful, but the trouble attending it laid the foundation of a heart complaint which some years later terminated fatally.

1790.

In this year the frigates " Orpheus," of 32 guns, and " Flora," of 36 guns, were extensively repaired in the Yard. On the 8th of November, the " Friendship " was launched, and on the 30th of November the Brunswick Dock was opened for the reception of shipping.

1791.

The " True Briton," of 800 tons, Captain Farrar, sailed on her first voyage to the Coast and China, Mr. Robert Wigram being the owner. She is reported to have sailed from the Downs, February 3rd, come to her moorings, May 20th, and to have made satisfactory earnings.

1793.

The East India Company's ship, " Warren Hastings," was launched. This ship became famous in the year 1806 on account of a most gallant action which she fought against the French frigate, " Piedmontese," and though at last the "Warren Hastings " was captured, the enemy was forced to haul off several times during the engagement, which lasted four hours. This ship was afterwards recaptured by the English.

1794.

The " Belliqueux," 64, built in the yard in 1778, is mentioned this year as taking part in the capture of San Domingo by Admiral Jervois, and in the same expedition the " Vesuvius " bomb vessel assisted at the taking of Martinique ; the affair was well planned and succeeded with but little loss of life.

This year, too,

When Howe, upon the 1st of June, put the Jacobin to flight,
And with old England's loud huzzas brought down their godless might,

he counted among his line of battle the " Theseus," 74, and if our vessel is

THE BRUNSWICK (Now the East India Export) Dock and Mast House.

Situated at the East end of Blackwall Yard, on the Thames.

for once not mentioned amongst those who took the lion's share of fighting, we do not find her named among a number who were held to have been conspicuously backward on that day. It was the greatest naval victory for many years, and a prelude to many still more glorious. Six French men of war were brought into Spithead, and the inhabitants who had never before seen such a sight, welcomed Lord Howe and his men as they deserved.

1795. The "Victorious," 74, built in the yard in 1783, was one of the squadron which this year took Simon's Bay from the Dutch ; this was rather a land than a sea action, and beyond disembarking men and guns the ships were not much engaged.

1796 At Blackwall, Mr. Perry's first wife, Elizabeth, died on the 25th of January at the age of forty-nine. A tablet to her memory in Poplar Chapel records "the goodness and sincerity of her heart and her parental and conjugal virtues."

On February 18th, 1796, George Green, who has already been referred to, and who at this time, by his perseverance and ability, had won for himself a position of considerable responsibility, was married to Mr. Perry's second daughter, Sarah.

The "Victorious," whom we last heard of at the Cape, reappears this year in Indian waters engaged in company with the "Arrogant," 74, with Admiral Sercey's fleet of six frigates. The action was severe, and both creditable and useful, and is interesting to read at length. The French outnumbered us in guns in the proportion of nineteen to eleven, and neither side had at the end much to boast of, the "Victorious" taking the "Arrogant" in tow, bore up for Madras, while Sercey's squadron found themselves equally in want of a refit, and were no more dangerous to our Indian commerce, an advantage we need hardly say of the utmost importance.

1797. We now arrive at a year unprecedented in the annals of our Blackwall fleet. The "Venerable," 74, flag ship to Admiral Duncan, was, we are pleased to note, one of the few vessels which took no share in the mutiny, either at Spithead or at the Nore ; on her deck Admiral Duncan made "the manly address to his crew which drew tears from the eyes of many;" indeed, we find her with only the "Adamant," 50, watching the Dutch fleet of fifteen sail of the line at the Texel, and keeping them at bay by repeated signals, as if to a fleet in the offing. Eventually, in June, being joined by thirteen sail of the line, including the "Belliqueux," they encountered the Dutch fleet off Camperdown. The details of this action are scarcely given with James's accus-

E 1

tomed fulness, but we learn that the "Venerable," leading the starboard division, engaged first the "Stadts General," whom she compelled to bear up, and then the Admiral's ship, the "Vryheid," to whose help came the "Brutus," "Leyden," and "Mars," and handled our ship severely, until she was relieved by the "Triumph," "Ardent," and "Director;" finally all three of the "Vryheid's" masts went by the board, and she, in company with ten more Dutch vessels surrendered. The feature of the action was that the enemy's fire was directed at the hulls of the English vessels rather than, as usual with the French and Spanish, at the rigging; our two vessels sustained their full share of casualties, which were on both sides severe. Turning now to the Mediterranean fleet, we have too much reason to fear that it was the discreditable conduct of her crew which detained the "Theseus" at Spithead, and deprived her of the honour of Cape St. Vincent. It is pleasant, however, to think that it was the same crew who now welcomed Sir Horatio Nelson with the following paper, placed anonymously on the quarter deck :— "Success attend Admiral Nelson! we will shed every drop of blood in our veins to support him, and the name of the 'Theseus' shall be immortalized as high as her captain's." Under this commander the "Theseus," in July of this year, aided at the bombardment of Cadiz, or rather of the Spanish fleet lying under the batteries of the town ; and in the barge of this vessel, with but fifteen men, Nelson encountered the Spanish commandant's armed launch with twenty-six ; it was a desperate hand-to-hand fight in the dark. "On this occasion," says Nelson, "my personal courage was more conspicuous than on any other in my life." Eighteen of the Spaniards were killed, the rest, including their commander, Don Miguel, wounded, and the launch taken. Direct from this affair the "Theseus" bore Nelson to the unfortunate attack upon "Teneriffe ;" baffled in the first attempt by contrary winds, he appears himself to have regarded the night attack as a forlorn hope, the enemy were perfectly prepared, and swept our boats with volleys of grape. Nelson himself never landed, but fell back into the launch with his arm shattered by a grape shot ; he was reconveyed to the "Theseus," and refused all help in climbing the side. In the cockpit of this vessel his arm was amputated.

From this long digression we must now return again to Blackwall Yard, where a change had been made in the constitution of the firm by the admission into partnership of Mr. Perry's two sons, John and Philip, and of his son-in-law, George Green ; the style of the firm, which had hitherto been John Perry and Co., had now become Perry, Sons, and Green.

1798.

The sister ships, "Kent" and "Ajax," both of 74 guns and 1931 tons, were built under Sir John Henslow, surveyor to the navy ; and the "Dragon," 74 guns and 1798 tons, was contracted for at £20 a ton. The "Dover Castle," East Indiaman, of 818 tons, was contracted for with J. Atkins, Esq., January 4th, at £17 a ton. The "Calcutta," East Indiaman, of 818 tons, for R. Charnock, Esq., on March 31st, at £17 a ton, and the "Bengal," East Indiaman, of 818 tons, on November 13th, at £16 a ton, for Gabriel Gillett, Esq.

Finding his health beginning to decline, and wishing to free himself from business, Mr. Perry in this year disposed of a moiety of the whole estate and business to Messrs. John Wells and William Wells the younger, of Bickley, Kent, as part of a partnership arrangement between himself and his sons, John and Philip, and his son-in-law, George Green, on the one part, and John and William Wells, junior, on the other part ; the style of the firm becoming, "Perry, Wells, and Green." Messrs. John and William Wells had from the year 1715 been very successful and well known shipbuilders at Deptford, occupying the premises now known as the Nelson Yard.

Afloat, the "Theseus" still remains the heroine of our story, though no longer bearing Admiral Nelson's flag, she was the fifth vessel to round the French fleet at the Battle of the Nile, and it was to her broadside that the "Guerrier's" already crippled mainmast fell ; then laying herself alongside the "Spartiate," she engaged that vessel (already occupied with the "Vanguard" and the "Aquilon"); these two vessels were among the first to strike their colours. Her loss of men in this action was slight, five killed and thirty wounded, but she had received more than seventy shots in her hull.

In the month of November we find the "Aurora" taking part with Admiral Duckworth's squadron in the capture of Minorca, accomplished with but little difficulty.

1799.

The "Theseus" in this year accompanied Sir Sidney Smith in the "Tigre" to the defence of Acre ; after landing a certain number of men to aid in the trenches, the duty of the ships was confined to annoying the enemy at each attack, and supporting any sortie ; unfortunately, quite towards the close of the siege, the bursting of some shells on the deck of the "Theseus" killed Captain Willett Miller, who had so long and so gallantly commanded this vessel, with forty of his crew. A monument to Captain Miller in St. Paul's Cathedral, displays the after-section of his ship, bearing the name of "Theseus" conspicuously on the stern.

At home, the "Lord Mornington," of 239 tons, was launched on January 24th, the contract price for building her being £11 per ton.

About this date Mr. Perry, having purchased the estate of Moor Hall, Harlow, married for his second wife Mary, the sister of his son-in-law, George Green, forming thus the double connection of father and brother-in-law. He was also this year appointed High Sheriff of the county, Mr. Pitt being especially desirous that able and independent men should hold these offices in the eastern counties.

1800.   April 10th, the "Travers," East Indiaman, of 571 tons, was contracted for with John Mangles, Esq., at £13 12s. 6d. a ton. April 31st, the "Skelton Castle," of 584 tons, with Hans Busk, Esq., at the same price : October 20th, the "Henry Addington," East Indiaman, of 1257 tons, was contracted for with Sir Alexander Hamilton, at £16 a ton; and the East Indiaman, "Alnwick Castle," of 1,200 tons, was launched.

1801.   April 1st, the "Agressor," "Archer," and "Bold," of 12 guns and 177 tons, were contracted for with the Government at £18 a ton. It was agreed that five shillings a ton extra should be paid on these vessels for every week that they should be completed within the contract time of four months.

The "Agressor" was completed in eleven weeks and three days, the "Archer" in eleven weeks and four days, and the "Bold" in thirteen weeks and four days.

In June of this year our fleet meets its first misfortune. Sir J. Saumerez, with seven sail of the line, made an attack on four French vessels protected by the batteries of Algeciras; the "Venerable" led the way followed by the rest of the fleet, including her sister the "Hannibal," but the wind was light, and the navigation difficult, and the whole affair, to say the least of it, a daring one. But little damage was done to the enemy, and the "Hannibal," we are sorry to say, went ashore under full fire of the batteries ; her captain was a true bit of stuff, and fought her to the last, but she eventually had to surrender with a loss of seventy-five killed and eighty wounded.

An earnest and by no means unsuccessful endeavour was made to retrieve this loss so soon as the French fleet quitted their anchorage ; the only part of it that concerns us is the hard set-to between the "Venerable" and "Formidable," 80 guns. The wind fell light, and the two engaged broadside to broadside, and within pistol shot, and after the cannonade had lasted an hour and a-half, the "Venerable's" mainmast came down (she had

VIEW OF THE EAST INDIA DOCKS.

begun the action under jury topmasts), and her enemy made her escape. Her loss in killed and wounded was 106.

Shortly afterwards, both fore and mizenmast went by the board, and the "Venerable" went ashore on the Spanish coast, but by great exertions was again got afloat, and being taken in tow by the "Thames," reached Gibraltar in safety.

We have no means of estimating to what extent our vessel had been crippled in her previous engagement; we have also James's statement that the relative force of the combatants was more than a third in favour of the Frenchman; still, to have effectually silenced the "Venerable" in so short a time is unquestionably, on paper, a good performance.

In October of this year the "Bonetta" was lost on the coast of Cuba, but we have no particulars except that the crew were saved.

1802. At Blackwall, the "Edward Foote," of 156 tons, was contracted for at the price of fourteen guineas a ton; and October 29th the "Experiment," East Indiaman, of 544 tons, at £19 a ton, with R. Taylor, Esq. The "Marchioness of Ely," East Indiaman, 1,016 tons, was also contracted for with John Locke, Esq.

1803. January 8th, the "Huddart," East Indiaman, of 544 tons, was contracted for at £19 a ton, with Captain John Woolmore; October 15th, the "Winchelsea," of 1,257 tons, at £19 a ton, with W. Moffat, Esq.; and the "Essex," East Indiaman, of 1,257 tons, at £19 a ton, with Henry Bonham, Esq. In this year Mr. Perry retired entirely from business. selling his remaining half of the yard and his interest in the business to Messrs. John and William Wells. The style of the firm remained as heretofore, Perry, Wells and Green, the partners being John Perry, Junr., Philip Perry, John Wells, William Wells, and George Green.

1804. On February 15th, 1804, was fought the celebrated action in the China Seas, when the East India Company's homeward bound China fleet, under Commodore Dance, beat off the French squadron. under Admiral Linois, which had come out with the intention of capturing or destroying at a single blow the whole of these valuable vessels. This action was ever after a just subject of pride to all connected with the East India Company's service, and to the whole mercantile marine of Great Britain. The ships under Commodore Dance's orders were the "Warley," "Royal George," "Coutts," "Wexford," "Alfred," "Ganges," "Exeter," "Henry Addington," "Hope," "Warren Hastings," "Dorsetshire," "Cumberland," "Earl of Abergavenny," and "Bombay Castle," with the country's ships, "Lord Castlereagh," "Carron," "Minerva," "David Scott," "Friendship," "Neptune," "Charlotte," and others. Most of these vessels had been either built or refitted in Blackwall Yard, where, no doubt, on such a notable occasion, the lively sympathy which was always shown for everything connected with the East India Company's service, must have blazed into a sort of reflected glory at the news of this brilliant success of these fighting Indiamen.

On July 25th, Messrs. Perry, Wells and Green contracted with the Government for three fir brigantines, the "Raven," "Saracen," and "Beagle," of 16 guns and 382 tons ; and about the same time a contract was entered into for the "Destruction" mortar vessel ; there were also in this year some heavy repairs effected to the "Belliqueux" and "Renommé." On November 24th the old "Venerable" was wrecked upon some sunken rocks in Torbay, the crew being, however, saved. The "Archer," 12 guns, is spoken of at this time as annoying the French shipping in Boulogne Harbour.

1805. The "Anibal," thus renamed by her captors, which had been so much battered in various engagements, was this year condemned by the French as unfit for further service. The "Victorious" and the "Crown" are only heard of at this period in Indian waters ; and the "Belliqueux" was probably still in Blackwall Yard undergoing repairs. The "Dragon" was engaged with Admiral Calder's squadron off Cape Finisterre, but singularly enough was the only ship unable to take any part in the action. She was subsequently despatched home with the prize "Dinow" in tow. While thus engaged, she was fallen in with by the van of the French fleet, and showed some promptitude in the way of deceiving the enemy by signals as to a fleet in the offing; one result of this service was, we presume, her absence from the battle of Trafalgar six weeks afterwards ; nor, we regret to say, can we report that any of the Blackwall ships, with the exception only of the "Africa," 64, were present on that glorious occasion. The "Africa's" doings on that day are sufficiently interesting. Having become separated from her consorts in the night, and mistaking in the morning Nelson's signal to make sail, she had to run the gauntlet of the fire from several of the enemy's vessels before laying herself, about 3 p.m., alongside the "Intrepide," a French 74 ; previously, however, she had sent a boat's crew to take possession of the dismasted "Santisima Trinidad," conceiving this vessel to have struck, and it was only when on her deck, that the lieutenant discovered his mistake, and was glad enough to be allowed to beat a retreat. The cannonade between our vessel and the "Intrepide" had lasted nearly three-quarters of an hour, when the timely arrival of the "Orion" compelled the latter to surrender. All the "Africa's" three lower masts were crippled, and she had several shots between wind and water, with a list of between sixty and seventy killed or wounded, proving, says James, that "considering Capt. Digby had voluntarily engaged so superior a force, although but a sixty-four, the "Africa" had performed as gallant a part as any vessel in the English line." The gun boat "Archer" took a prominent part this April in the capture of a number of French transports loaded with stores from the camp at Ostende

In this year Mr. Perry added the sum of £250 to the charitable bequest of his father already mentioned, making up the sum to £450 consols, the interest of which is still given to the poor of Poplar. He also, at this time, presented a new organ to Poplar Chapel. We have here to record, on May 18th, 1805, the premature death, at Blackwall, of Mrs. George Green, at the early age of 28 years : her son John, aged 9 years, dying on the following day, they were buried together, with the other members of her family, in the grounds of Poplar Chapel. She left two sons, George and Richard, but of these only Richard Green arrived at maturity.

In Mr. Perry's time Blackwall Yard attained to its greatest area ; it extended along the north bank of the river Thames from Blackwall Stairs to the entrance to the river Lea, at Bow Creek, and backwards for nearly a quarter of a mile, to where the boundary wall now stands which divides the export from the import basin of the East India Docks ; along this side, the boundary road was adorned with lines of trees, which formed in summer a most delightful public promenade.

It may here be stated that Mr. Perry played a noiseless but effective part during the great war. The regiments ordered on foreign service used to go down to Blackwall, where they embarked on board their transports, and at such times Mr. Perry was frequently enabled to give the Government much assistance and many facilities. He was often brought into contact with Mr. Pitt, to whom he was a devoted adherent as well as an attached friend ; he had also business relations with his brother, the Earl of Chatham, who was for some time First Lord of the Admiralty, and with many other exalted personages, including King George himself.

Mr. Perry was a man of considerable eloquence, and Mr. Green used to relate how, on one occasion, he went to a public meeting, and there found the audience strongly opposed to his views. He spoke only a few words, but they were quite sufficient to turn the tables and to bring his hearers round to the same opinions as himself.

F

The following has also been recorded of him by his son, the late Mr. Richard Perry, in a short biography contained in his "Contributions to an Amateur Magazine":—"At a Middlesex election, Mr. Perry proposed Mr. Mainwaring in opposition to Sir Francis Burdett; when he came forward on the hustings the mob hooted and called him a Government contractor. 'Yes,' replied he, 'I contract with the Government to build ships. I built, for instance, the "Venerable," which was Lord Duncan's flag ship at the battle of Camperdown. I built such and such a ship,' mentioning various other famous vessels and the victorious battles in which they had been engaged. He had touched a true chord of national feeling; the people began to cheer and he sat down in a tempest of applause."

King George, it is related, was very fond of inspecting the embarkation of his troops, and would at such times ask Mr. Perry many very pertinent questions. On one of these occasions, when at Blackwall in the middle of summer inspecting some cavalry before a large number of spectators, it is said that a "jolly tar," rather more than "three sheets in the wind," though brim full of loyalty," and consequently regardless of all rules of etiquette or decorum, ventured to approach "His Majesty's royal person" with a full quart of humble porter, which he had just brought from a neighbouring ale-house. Jack, to use nautical phraseology, "tongued his quid," "unshipped his sky-scraper," "hitch'd up his canvas," and hoped his Majesty would not refuse to drink with a "true blue." The King, as may be supposed, was for a moment astounded at the impudence of the sailor, but Jack was not to be beat off, and a second time importuned His Majesty to "take a sup." The King, finding that the remonstrances of his courtiers were useless, good humouredly took the jug from the hands of the tar, and gave, for a toast, "The Army and the Navy," partaking at the same time of the invigorating beverage; then, returning the remains to Jack with "a coin of the realm," desired him to join with his shipmates in drinking success to the campaign and long life to the King and Queen.

So courteous was the old King to Mr. Perry on all occasions, that at last he was jokingly styled among Mr. Perry's intimates "The friend of the family." Mr. Green used also to relate with much satisfaction how, on one of the King's visits to Blackwall, he had the honour of buckling on His Majesty's spurs.

On one occasion, when the Prince of Wales had come down to the yard on some official business, Mr. Perry was severely mortified that he did not show him the same kindly consideration as his Royal father. A

splendid collation had been prepared for the Prince, but he merely entered the room, walked once round the table, coldly refusing to take any refreshments, and then left the house, leaving Mr. Perry in a most indignant frame of mind. Mr. Perry's career was throughout marked by extreme liberality and by a magnanimous and public spirit. It is said, but we do not know on what authority, that on one occasion he presented the country with a ship of war completely equipped. His family believed that he might have obtained a peerage, and he is stated to have refused a baronetcy.

Like Mr. Gladstone, at the present time, Mr. Perry had a great idea of hewing down trees, and his son Richard writes :—" I think I see my father now, with his face slightly elevated and beaming with intelligence (he was one the handsomest men of the day), issuing from his hall door armed with a saw or bill-hook attached to a long pole by way of handle, with which he operated on the top branches of the lofty trees, and making his way into one of the plantations, from whence, soon after, was heard the grinding of the saw or the blows on some huge bough."

" Travelling from Blackwall to Harlow, Mr. Perry's road lay through Epping Forest, which was considered both a long and dangerous journey. Mr. Perry drove this with his own horses, and frequently stopped to dine at Woodford ; he always took his own wine with him, but at the same time he made a point of paying at the inn for the amount which he might be supposed to have consumed. In the neighbourhood of Woodford he had a great friend, Sir Robert Preston, a large shipowner and Deputy Master of the Trinity House, who used to send him the dessert for his dinner." This Sir Robert Preston was said to have been one of the founders of the Ministerial whitebait dinner.

By his first marriage, Mr. Perry had four sons and four daughters, the two eldest sons, John and Philip, who were partners at Blackwall, retired from business at their father's death, and died some years afterwards unmarried. The third son, Thomas, went to India in the Civil Service, and was in due course succeeded by his son, the present Mr. John Perry-Watlington, who, after the death of his wife's father added to his own name his wife's family name of Watlington. Mr. John Perry-Watlington, as already mentioned, is the present head of the Perry family. He sat for some years in the House of Commons as the Conservative member for South Essex. Mr. Perry's second daughter, Sarah, as already stated, was married to Mr. George Green.

By his second marriage, with Miss Green, Mr. Perry had six

children. Of these, the eldest, Richard, was a scholar of Trinity College, Cambridge, and has already been referred to as the author of a pleasant little book, entitled "Contributions to an Amateur Magazine." George was a clergyman, and died leaving a widow and family; Mary Anne, now Mrs. Savage, a widow; and Charles, now Bishop Perry, are still living. The latter, who took the high degree of Senior Wrangler, and seventh in the first class in the classical tripos, was, in 1847, selected to fill the difficult and responsible position of Bishop of the newly-formed see of Melbourne, which he held for more than twenty-seven years, beloved by all classes of society, and honoured and respected for his moderation, his sincerity, and his conciliatory disposition, even by those whose feelings on religious subjects were different from his own. One daughter died an infant, and the youngest, Amelia, was for many years known at Blackwall as a most active, regular, and intelligent member of the managing committee of her uncle George Green's Schools, for which she maintained the deepest interest until her death in 1874.

Mr. Perry died at Battersea, on the 7th of November, 1810, at the age of sixty-seven, and was buried with his wife in the family vault at Poplar Chapel. The following lines inscribed on his monument are worth recording :—

> " If private worth, combined with public zeal,
> Demand a tribute of the love we feel ;
> If honor, truth, nobility conspire
> To form examples which the just admire,
> This frail memorial may awhile suspend
> The swift oblivion that succeeds our end ;
> Preserve some record for the stranger's eye
> Of generous virtues that should never die,
> Of active merits mixed with ardent mind,
> Which made his own the good of human kind,
> Diffus'd around the bounty Heaven bestows,
> And sooth'd the sharpness of malignant woes ;
> The poor attest it, whom he clothed and fed,
> The sick he nourished on their dying bed ;
> The friends he succour'd, and the youth he reared,
> To Christian hope by Christian promise cheered ;
> In deeds like these, revere his honor'd name,
> In Brunswick Dock his arduous skill proclaim
> That bold achievement of his useful toil
> Which bless'd with consequence his native soil,
> First taught this humble spot with wealth to smile,
> And rise Emporium of the British Isle ;
> May such benevolence, from Earth removed,
> Await its destiny from God he loved,
> Celestial grace and mercy guard his tomb,
> And endless glory seal his final doom."

Chapter Ⅴ.

About this time, Messrs. John and William Wells sold some pieces of land at Blackwall to the new East India Dock Company, and in February, 1805, they arranged with Mr. Robert Wigram, whose name has been already mentioned, and who by this time had become largely interested in shipping, for the sale to him of "All those several pieces or parcels of ground, including the Great Dockyard and other yards, docks, gardens and grounds, and the capital messuage or mansion house, and other houses, launches, storehouses, warehouses, workshops, coach-houses, stables, sheds, and other erections and buildings. &c., &c., &c., situate at Blackwall, &c."

In June of this year, only a few months previous to the battle of Trafalgar, the Government had contracted with the firm of Messrs. Perry, Wells and Green, for the construction of three new line of battle ships, the "Magnificent," 74 guns and 1,731 tons ; the "Elizabeth," 74 guns and 1,723 tons, and the "Valiant," 74 guns and 1,718 tons, at the price of £36 a ton.

The "Magnificent," 74, was launched in September, 1806, that is within fifteen months after the contract had been signed, and the East India Company's ship "Britannia" of 1,273 tons, was also launched about the same time. In this year also, Mr. Perry disposed of his Brunswick Dock to the East India Dock Company, which had been formed for the purpose of purchasing this and constructing what is now known as the East India Import Dock. In January and May of this year, Sir Robert Wigram's two sons, Money and Henry Loftus, came to reside in the yard, at the respective ages of sixteen and fifteen.

The "Valiant," 74, was launched eighteen months, and the "Elizabeth," 74, twenty-one months after the contract for them had been signed. The "Valiant" was at once commissioned with all possible speed in time to join Admiral Gambier's fleet in August. The object of the expedition was to demand the surrender of the Danish fleet, it was important therefore, to move before the winter closed the Baltic ; their end was obtained, but the affair, says James, "was not one from which much glory could be reaped." The "Elizabeth" made her first cruise to Lisbon where she assisted in the blockade of the Tagus, a precautionary measure which influenced the hesitating Portuguese Government to make common cause with the English.

1808.   On January 21st, 1808, Henry Green, the eldest child of Mr. Green's second marriage, was born at Blackwall. The "Theseus," 74, is again employed with the Mediterranean Squadron chasing the French fleet into Toulon. The annals of the East India Company record this year the loss of no fewer than four of their outward and ten of their homeward bound vessels; two new ships were, however, launched at Blackwall for their chartered fleet, viz., the "Warren Hastings" of 1,200 tons, J. Larkins, Esq., Managing Owner, and the "Carnatic" of 822 tons, W. Agnew, Esq., Managing Owner. The "Cherokee" and the "Leveret" of 10 guns and 237 tons were also launched for the Government.

1809.   The "Ajax" and "Berwick" of 74 guns and 1,760 tons were launched this year. The "Theseus" and "Valiant" being mentioned as taking part in Lord Gambier's action in the Basque Roads, and the "Victorious" as accompanying Sir R. J. Strachan to the Scheldt and taking part in the bombardment of Flushing.

1810.   The "Ajax" was commissioned and joined the blockading squadron off Toulon, where she exchanged shots with her French namesake. Subsequently she was a good deal knocked about in a cutting out expedition at Palamos. The "Valiant," however, was more fortunate, and made prize of the French armed merchant vessel "Confiance," with a cargo from the Isle of France, valued at £150,000. The "Magnificent," with one or two smaller vessels, captured the island of Santa Anna. At Blackwall the "America," 74 guns, and 1,758 tons, was launched, as well as the "Rose," East Indiaman, of 955 tons, the "Guildford," of 506 tons, and the "Cæsar," of 604 tons.

1811.   The "Ajax" captured a French twenty gun vessel of 800 tons, loaded with shot and shell for Corfu. The "Berwick" chased the new French 44 gun frigate "Amazone" into shoal water in the Channel, where she was fired by her own crew. The "Magnificent" still continued with Admiral Pellew off Toulon. At Blackwall the following ships were launched:—The "Cabalva," East Indiaman, of 1,267 tons, for W. Davies, Esq.; the "Prince Regent," East Indiaman, of 952 tons, for Henry Bonham, Esq.; the "Bengal," East Indiaman, of 955 tons, for G. Gillett, Esq.; and the "Barham," 74 guns, and 1760 tons, for the Government. Of this ship a peculiar memorial has been preserved. On the day, probably, of her launch some idle draughtsman wrote on one of the windows of the

Mould Loft with a diamond—" Barham, 74, 1811."—Singularly enough the frail glass has outlasted the oak and iron of the ship and the bricks and mortar of the Mould Loft, for the pane was rescued by the present Mr. Robert Wigram, nearly seventy years afterwards, when the Mould Loft was being taken down by the Midland Railway Company, and still remains as an interesting relic in Messrs. Wigram's possession.

1812. On the 3rd of March, 1812, Sir Robert Wigram's son, John, was killed at Walthamstow by a fall from his gig. On the 12th of August the whole of the Blackwall Yard estate became vested in Sir Robert Wigram. At this time, Mr. William Wells having retired, the partners in the firm were Sir Robert Wigram, holding six-sixteenth shares, Mr. John Wells, holding four-sixteenth shares, Mr. George Green, holding four-sixteenth shares, and Mr. John Wigram, holding two-sixteenth shares. The style of the firm was Wigram, Wells and Green. The " Pembroke," 74 guns, and 1,758 tons was launched. The amount of business done this year both in building and repairing had been very large, everything appears to have gone well, and the profits are said to have been very considerable.[*] Money and Loftus Henry Wigram were now brought into the business in place of their late brother. The new seventy-four gunship "America" had been sent to the Mediterranean, where she drove a French ship of equal size under shelter of the Island of St. Margueritte. The " Magnificent," with a new "Venerable," swept along the coast of Spain, making daring attacks on the enemy's posts wherever opportunity allowed. In this way they carried Le Quentin, in a very dashing manner, and also Santander. The " Victorious" was watching, off Venice, the French 74 gun ship, " Tivoli," building at that port. The " Tivoli," when completed, put to sea and, finding escape doubtful, did not decline the battle. The combatants were well matched in size, number of guns, and men, and it was not until after five hours of "tremendous cannonade" that the main mast of the " Tivoli" went by the board.

Meantime the little " Leverett," 10 guns, with the " Brittomart," sister ship, had carried in their boats, a French privateer of 14 guns; the action occurred off Heligoland, and is described as a " very spirited enterprize;" but the feat of the year we presume must be taken to be the way in which Captain J. Hayes saved his vessel, the " Magnificent," then on her return to England, when caught in a sudden storm off the French coast.

[*] See Appendix.

The precise manœuvre we shall not attempt to describe, suffice to say, that it was performed "in a manner so extraordinary and so creditable to the skill and presence of mind of the Captain that we feel it a duty thus to mention it."

1813.   This year the new ship "Pembroke," 74 guns, joined the blockade off Toulon, while the "Berwick" and "Elizabeth" continued their reconaissance of the coast, and did a good deal of damage. The "Valiant" was employed watching the Americans in Chesapeake Bay, and the little "Bold," 12 guns, was wrecked on Prince Edward's Island. About this time the Government, freed by Nelson's victories from danger in European waters, found itself hard pressed by the large American 40 gun frigates, such as the "Chesapeake," so well remembered from her contest with the English frigate "Shannon." To meet this difficulty, orders were given for the rapid construction of forty fir frigates, popularly known as the "Forty Thieves," ten of these—

The "Cydnus" of 38 guns and 1,078 tons.

"Eurotas"	38	,,	1,080	,,
"Niger"	38	,,	1,066	,,
"Severn"	40	,,	1,258	,,
"Forth"	40	,,	1,251	,,
"Liffey"	40	,,	1,261	,,
"Glasgow"	40	,,	1,259	,,
"Liverpool"	40	,,	1,246	,,
"Newcastle"	50	,,	1,556	,,
"Leander"	50	,,	1,571	,,

were built in Blackwall Yard; a painting of the yard, with several of these vessels on the stocks, is now at Blackwall, in the possession of Messrs. Green, and is here given. These were the last ships built for the Government in connection with the great naval wars of the early part of this century. The profits of the years 1813—14 are again reported as having been very satisfactory. Mr. John Wells had retired and disposed of his quarter of the business to Sir Robert Wigram, and the partners in the firm of Wigrams and Green, as it was now styled, were Sir Robert Wigram, holding one-half, George Green, one-quarter, and Money and Henry Loftus Wigram, one-eighth each.

About this time a hideous land-mark stood on the south bank of the Thames, just below Blackwall Point, facing the entrance of the river Lea; this was a cross-headed gibbet, from which hung in chains the bodies of

BLACKWALL YARD, 1813

four pirates, who having undergone the extreme penalty of the law at Execution Dock, had been removed to Blackwall Point, to serve as a solemn warning to all passers by.

1814.   The Honourable East India Company's packet, "St. Helena," of 136 tons, and the "Lady Melville," of 1,263 tons, were launched this year, and the private books show that the business must have been in a highly prosperous condition. At this time the firm of Wigrams and Green had already become largely interested in ship owning, and held shares in the following vessels:—The "Warley," "Glatton," "Neptune," "Carnatic," "Coutts," "Cabalva," "Huddart," "Earl Spencer," "Surat Castle," "Rose," "Cæsar," "Hope," "Lady Melville," "Marchioness of Ely," "Bengal," "Prince Regent," "Ceres," "Charlton," and "Travers." To return to the Blackwall ships of war, the "Berwick" is reported off Toulon, as engaged in a running fight. The "Forty Thieves," though barely in commission, soon began to give the enemy a taste of their quality.

"Among the means," says James, "taken to meet the American frigates on equal terms, some of the British 38-gun class were mounted with medium 24 pounders and allowed an increased complement of men. The first two so fitted were the 'Cydnus' and 'Eurotas,' both built of red pine and recently launched." A long account is given of this plan of armament, which was highly approved of by the officers at the Nore, nor was it long ere its efficiency was put to the test, for before the "Eurotas" had been many weeks at sea she encountered the French 40-gun frigate "Clorinde," her equal in size and number of crew. Here again the description of this action should be read at length. It was a question of which could stay longest and smite hardest. Night fell on an undecided action, and at dawn, much to the regret of the biographer, the approach of a second English vessel deprived the "Eurotas" of the glory of an unaided victory. At the same time almost to a day the "Niger," with the "Tagus," also 40 guns, captured the "Ceres," a Frenchman of equal size, while the "Severn," then convoying merchantmen to Bermuda, escaped from a two days' running fight with two Frenchmen without injury. We hear of this vessel again in

1816.   Chesapeake Bay, and again, in 1816, with the "Glasgow" at the battle of Algiers, this latter vessel suffering severely from a raking fire from the shore.

1817.   At home the East India Company's ship "Waterloo," of 1,325 tons, was launched, and in the following year the East India Company's ship

G

1818.   " Canning " of 1,326 tons, the " Duke of York," East Indiaman, of 1,327
tons, Stewart Majoribanks, Esq., managing owner, and the " Dunira," East
Indiaman, of 1,325 tons, George Palmer, Esq., managing owner, were
launched. It may also be interesting to record here that on June 16th, 1817,
an Act for making the hamlet of Poplar and Blackwall a distinct parish, and
for erecting a parish church, received the royal assent.

1819.   The " Catherine," of 535 tons, was launched and chartered by the
Company, and on August 23rd Sir Robert Wigram retired from active
business and sold the whole of the Blackwall Yard estate to George Green,
Money Wigram, and Henry Loftus Wigram for £40,500, Mr. Green taking
half and the two Messrs. Wigrams a quarter each.

Sir Robert Wigram having now retired, this may be considered a
fitting opportunity to introduce the following sketch of his life and
family, which has been contributed by his grandson, the present Mr.
Robert Wigram.

THE WIGRAM FAMILY has been stated to be of some considerable antiquity in Ireland, and a certain amount of evidence has been
produced in support of this view. However this may be, it is clear that
when, January 30th, 1744, Robert Wigram was born at Wexford, their
fortunes were at a low ebb.

His father, John Wigram, master of the privateer " Boyne," married,
in 1742, his cousin, Mary Clifford, and was lost or died at sea 1746, without, it
is believed, ever seeing his son. The widow's means were small, and when
eighteen years of age young Robert arrived in London with but £200 and
an introduction to Dr. Allen, an eminent physician, whose descendants at
this moment occupy a good position in Sydney. He found in him a kind
and true friend who took him as his apprentice, and in two years Robert
Wigram, having taken his diploma as surgeon, sailed for India in the East
India Company's ship " Admiral Watson," February 20th, 1764. When on
board this vessel a friendship, which lasted their mutual lives, was formed
with William Taylor Money, then second officer of the same ship. March
2nd, 1768, he sailed as surgeon of the " Duke of Richmond," and in the
same capacity on board the " British King " in 1770.

On returning from this voyage, he the same year, December 19th,
married Catherine Brodhurst of Mansfield, and becoming disqualified by an
attack of ophthalmia contracted in China, for his profession of surgeon, and

having, to quote his own words, "gained a perfect knowledge of the trade of India and China, I had great advantages as a drug merchant."

"The Dutch and Germans being furnished with most of their drugs from London, my great knowledge turned my little capital to very great advantage, and I afterwards became a general merchant over the whole world, a brewer, shipbuilder, India husband, (charterer of ships to the East India Company) and great promoter of Huddart's patent for hemp cables."

"On my first marriage and commencing the mercantile line, my capital did not exceed £3,000. We lived at this time in Union Court and, subsequently, in White Lion Court. Catherine Wigram died January 22, 1786."

Mr. Wigram took Walthamstow House in 1782, and on June 3rd, 1787, married Eleanor, daughter of John Watts, Secretary to the Victualling Office.

He would appear to have made his first venture in shipowning by buying in 1788 the "Gen. Goddard," 799 tons, and he then built at Mr. Well's yard at Deptford, the "True Briton," 1,198 tons, launched November 13th, 1790, which like the former vessel he chartered to the East India Company; this Company, it is hardly necessary to remark, had, at this date, a monopoly of the trade to the East, and supplemented their own fleet with vessels chartered from private owners. From the pages of "Hardy's Register," therefore, a book by-the-bye well worth the study of anyone curious in old City names, we are able to collect a pretty exact list of Robert Wigram's East India fleet, which appear at the following dates :—

"London"	...	...	836 Tons, 1792—3
"Rockingham"	... ...	798 ,,	1793—4
"Lascelles"	... ...	824 ,,	

Early in the year 1793 the long war between England and France, which only finally terminated in 1815, was declared. The revolutionary armies invaded Belgium and Holland, which had sided with England, while the allies, Austria, Prussia, and England, opposed them there and on the German frontier. Fortune, however, for the present, was unfavourable. The Austrians and Prussians retired : the Dutch, with the Duke of York's army, were behind the Waal. During the winter Pichegrou crossed that river on the ice, surprised, and became master of the country and fleet. The Prince of Orange escaped to England, and the Revolutionary Party in Holland made a treaty with France, and thus became involved in the war

G I

with England. The news of this change reached St. Helena while Robert
Wigram's vessel, the "Gen. Goddard," was waiting for convoy on her fifth
voyage, and her captain, William Taylor Money, determined to join in an
attempt to intercept the Dutch Fleet expected from Batavia. Fitting (at
the expense, we conclude, of his owner and friend) the "Gen. Goddard"
with thirty guns, he started on a cruise with H.M.'s ship "Sceptre," 64 guns,
and the "Swallow Packet," "Asia," and "Busbridge," East Indiamen. He
was the first to sight the Dutch Fleet and to give chase. He came up to
them in the night, and at daybreak captured seven of them, the other vessels
of the squadron not being near enough to take any decided part in the
action. Extraordinary as this story is, it is, nevertheless, undoubtedly true,
and appears to have met with the full approval of his owner, who had a
picture painted of the action, which is now in the possession of Mrs.
Money Wigram, at Moor Place, Herts. The share of prize-money allotted
to the five vessels exceeded £61,000. Captain Money received a vote of
thanks and a sword from the merchants at St. Helena in testimony of their
appreciation of his conduct.

In 1794, Sir John Jervis and Sir Charles Grey, starting from
Barbadoes, took Martinique and some forts in St. Lucia and Guadaloupe.
The French made various attempts to recover these islands, and a large
expedition was sent from Portsmouth, in January, 1796, which resulted in
subduing a revolt in Grenada, and the capture of St. Lucia and Demerara.
During some of these operations the Government, having determined to
send troops to the West Indies, had pressing need of transports, and
Robert Wigram, knowing of the want of ships, immediately bought four—
the "Pershore," "Valentine," "Gen. Elliot," and "Contractor"—hired them
to the Government as transports, fitted them out, and had them ready for
sea in a wonderfully short time. His activity in getting these vessels ready
was so great that for several weeks, says Mrs. Wigram, "we breakfasted at
four or five in the morning." A picture of these vessels leaving Spithead
in 1795 is now at Esher Place, Money Wigram's, Esq.

To return to "Hardy," we find at this time belonging to
R. Wigram :—

		Tons.	
" Woodcot "	...	802	1796—7
" Walpole "	...	774	1797—8
" Contractor " ...	...	777	Returned apparently from her West India trip.
" Walthamstow "	...	820	1799

	Tons.	
" Lady Jane Dundas "	820	
" Windham " ...	... 820	1800—1
" Marquis of Ely " ...	... 1,200	1801—2
" Tottenham "	... 517	
" Wexford "	... 1,200	1802—3
" Retreat " ...	 505	1805—6
" Woodford "	... 1,180	1806— 7

December 19th, 1802, Mr. Wigram began his parliamentary life, being returned as member for Fowey, in Cornwall.

He was, from the first, a great admirer of Mr. Pitt, and one night that minister having spoken strongly on some subject of importance, and being deeply grieved at the adverse vote which followed, as he was leaving the House a few members, Robert Wigram amongst the number, rose and attended him to the door. Mr. Pitt looking round to note his friends asked, " Who was the little man in shorts ? " and subsequently, October 30th, 1805, created him a baronet.

There is more than one night in 1803—4 to which this story may refer, or possibly to the impeachment of Lord Melville, April 1805, when history relates that Pitt's tears were concealed by his friends.

November of this year he was elected member for his native town of Wexford, which he had left forty-four years before, with £200 in his pocket.

In this year also he arranged the purchase of the Blackwall Yard Estate from Messrs. J. & W. Wells, together with a considerable quantity of adjacent land.

The list of the yard fleet, that is the ships owned by the firm of Wigrams and Green, in all of which Sir Robert had an interest, is given in another place. With his partnerships in Blackwall Yard, in Reid's Brewery, Huddart's Rope Works, together with his own business in Crosby Square, where for many years he resided, and as Chairman of the new East India Docks, opened in 1810, he must have had enough upon his hands. He was also getting on in years, and at sixty-six, the indomitable spirit which had so long and through so many difficulties commanded success, would naturally be seeking repose. The precise date of his leaving the House of Commons is uncertain, but it was previous to 1817 when his name appears at the head of a loyal memorial, signed by 3,000 of the principal merchants of London (protesting against the recent outrage against the sacred person of the Prince Regent). He placed sons both in the Brewery and at Blackwall, but appears to have made no effort to keep up his business as merchant, which probably died a natural death. His successor in the ropery was William Cotton, late Governor of the Bank of England. He resided the latter part of his life at his place at Walthamstow, where he died, November 6th, 1830.

It was his practice on certain days every week to visit the yard at Blackwall and the Ropeworks at Limehouse, and as he rode along, accompanied by six or seven of his sons, all well mounted, and fine handsome men, he commanded the admiration of the neighbourhood. Of his large family, twenty-three (or as he liked to phrase it twice two-and-twenty) nearly all attained to man's estate, and most to a good old age, the best known being William, immortalized by Macaulay as "the most obstinate of the East India Directors," and many years Master of the Puckeridge foxhounds; Joseph Cotton, Bishop of Rochester; James, Vice-Chancellor; Loftus, Q.C., and member for the University of Cambridge.

The present head of the family is General Sir Frederick Wellington Fitzwigram, Bart., of Leigh Park, Hants.

But few anecdotes remain either of Sir Robert's later years or of his earlier struggles. The prettiest, to our mind, is that which tells how his mother, who used to spend her time, during her husband's long absence in his vessel, in working for the poor of her native town, would reply to their expressions of thankfulness: "Pray not only for me, but for my little boy and his father at sea." She lived to see and share the boy's prosperity.

Dr. Allan's rough though kind advice on his first arrival in London may also be mentioned. "You are come, young man, to a place where, if you tumble down, no one will pick you up."

"I always," says Sir Robert, speaking of that time of his life, "lived respectably; and as I had no opportunity of making acquaintance whom I could value, I made none."

"I never did undertake any business of moment without consultation with my wife, and can truly say it has much promoted my fortune."

Whatever may be thought of the foregoing, his advice to his large family will be at least approved of—"Remember the strength of the bundle of sticks."

Though a bold adventurer in all legitimate branches of commerce, he had a wholesome old-fashioned dread of speculation, and of one commercial danger we find him speaking with a kind of horror. "How near I was, by Addington's loan, of completely ruining the old house."

His objection to banking—" I never will have to do with a business where I must mistrust those with whom I have to deal"—seems to us founded on a misapprehension.

His portraits represent a man of strong common sense, with a good-humoured, kindly expression, and with plenty of firmness and individuality.

His life would be, perhaps, hardly complete without some mention of his confidential clerk, Mr. Hewison, to whose unremitting attention he attributed much of his success, and whose son is still serving his grandsons with equal integrity and ability. On one year, when there was every reason to believe that the profits would be exceptionally large, there was an unaccountable unwillingness and delay in producing the accounts, and when the reason for this was inquired into, " Sir," replied Mr. Hewison, " I never knew a man make so much one year but he was sure to knock it all down the next."

Chapter VI.

1820.

The ships in which the firm was interested at this time were the " Ferrers," " Timmins," " Hope," " Minerva," " Vansittart," " Princess Charlotte of Wales," " Duke of York," " Surat Castle," " Rose," " Cæsar," " Lady Melville," " Prince Regent," and " Marchioness of Ely." The sister ships, " Repulse " and " Royal George," East Indiamen, of 1,333 tons, were launched for J. F. Timmins, Esq., and the " Hope," of 434 tons. On November 6th the " Kent," East Indiaman, of 1,332 tons, was launched for Stewart Majoribanks, Esq. The destruction of this last-named ship by fire in the Bay of Biscay, on March 1st, 1825, when on her third voyage to India with troops under the command of Captain Cobb, is no doubt already a familiar story to most of our readers.

1821.

The shadow of a coming change appears at Blackwall during this year, in the form of the first steam vessel yet constructed in the yard. This was the paddle-wheel steamer, " City of Edinboro'," of 401 tons, launched for the Edinboro' Steam Navigation Company, March 31st, 1821, about ten years before this time the paddle-wheel steamer "Comet" had already been constructed on the Clyde. The " Duchess of Athol," East Indiaman, of 1,333 tons, was also launched for W. E. Ferrers, Esq.

On the 29th of March, 1821, the first stone of the new Parish Church of Poplar was laid by the Bishop of London. An imposing procession was formed, consisting of the Bishop, the Directors of the

East and West India Dock Companies, and a great number of the leading inhabitants. On this occasion the learned rector, the Rev. Samuel Hoole, is reported to have given a most impressive address. The architect of this church was Mr. C. Hollis, and the builder Mr. Thomas Morris of Poplar. The church was consecrated July 3rd, 1823.

1822.

In this year, Henry Green, the second son of George Green, Esq., was in accordance with old custom, apprenticed to his father as a shipwright, at the age of fourteen, his elder brother Richard being at this time in Edinburgh, where he studied for several years at the University. The paddle-wheel steamer, "King of the Netherlands," 180 tons, was launched for the General Steam Navigation Company, and on April 24th, the "Sir Edward Paget," of 458 tons, was launched for Messrs. Meaburn and Johnson.

1823.

The paddle wheel steamers "Harlequin" and "Cinderella," of 244 tons were, launched for the General Steam Navigation Company, and the paddle wheel steamer "Soho," of 510 tons, for the Edinboro' Steam Navigation Company.

1824.

The following ships were launched, the "Surat Castle," of 1,223 tons; the "Lord Amherst," of 506 tons, for Messrs. Johnson and Meaburn; the paddle wheel steamer "Queen of the Netherlands," of 159 tons, for the General Steam Navigation Company; the "Columbia" and "Pearl," of 251 tons; the "Simon Taylor," of 408 tons, on which vessel Henry Green was appointed to act as assistant foreman, and the "Carn Brae Castle," of 570 tons. This last named ship, in which the firm held an interest, was designed by Captain Huddart, and managed by Messrs. Huddart Brothers for Captain Davey, an old East India Company's officer. She was altogether a new type of ship, being the first expressly built for the passenger trade to Calcutta, and was considered the finest vessel of the day. She was subsequently lost in Freshwater Bay, Isle of Wight, on the afternoon of the day she left Portsmouth, by standing too close in to the land, while the captain and passengers were at dinner. In this year also, the "Sir Edward Paget," was purchased by Mr. Green, and became noteworthy, as the first ship of Messrs. Green's well-known passenger line to India and Australia. The "Sir Edward Paget," or the "Paget," as she was generally called, was a very smart ship and most elaborately fitted, as became the first vessel of the new line. She was commanded by Captain Geary of the Royal Navy, and carried a square white flag with St. George's red cross through the centre. On her arrival at

Spithead, the Admiral of the port sent his lieutenant off to ask what ship was carrying an Admiral's flag, and on learning that it was a merchant vessel, he ordered it to be at once hauled down. The story goes, that a blue handkerchief was then sewn on the centre of the flag, and the lieutenant having satisfied himself that naval regulations were no longer being infringed, it was allowed to be rehoisted, and continued the distinguishing flag of all the Blackwall ships until the firm was some years afterwards divided. On her return home after the first voyage, the "Sir Edward Paget" was brought up off the Yard, and on Mr. Green's proceeding on board to make the usual inspection, he was much to his dismay received with manned yards and a salute, the ship's band playing "The Conquering Hero"; this reception, together with the man-of-war like appearance of everything he saw on board so astonished Mr. Green that he was by no means surprised to learn, when the voyage accounts were balanced, that this man-of-war like style, however imposing it might be, was not financially successful, and, we need scarcely add that the captain and the regulations of the ship throughout were changed before the second voyage.

1825.   The "Roxburgh Castle," of 565 tons, was next launched for the firm, and chartered on her first voyage by the East India Company for China and Quebec ; Captain George Denny was appointed commander, and the present Captain Edward Hight served as a midshipman on board. The "Abercrombie Robinson," of 1,325 tons, and the "Edinburgh," of 1,325 tons, were launched for Henry Bonham, Esq., and in this year Henry Green left Blackwall for a time, and joined the East India Company's ship, "Vansittart," Captain Dalrymple, as fifth officer, sailing for the Cape of Good Hope, Bombay, and China.

1826.   A steam vessel of 279 tons was launched for the Honourable Corporation of the Trinity House, and the "Prince Rupert," of 229 tons, for the Hudson's Bay Company.

1827.   The "Sir J. Cockburn," of 340 tons, and the "Thames," of 370 tons, were launched, and in this year Henry Green went for a second voyage to the Cape, Bombay, and China on board the East India Company's ship, "Charles Grant," commanded by Captain William Hay. Over four acres of land belonging to the Yard were at this time sold to the East and West India Dock Company. The "Boyne," of 619 tons, was purchased by Mr. George Green.

1828.   The "Sir John Rae Reid," of 300 tons, was launched for Messrs. Reid, Irving and Company, and the "Lady Raffles," of 549 tons, was

H

purchased by Mr. George Green, Captain W. Tucker being appointed to the command.

1829.   In this year Richard Green, the eldest son of Mr. George Green, who had been in the Yard for some time since his return from Edinburgh, was admitted into partnership at the age of twenty-six, and undertook the management of the ships belonging to his father and the firm. In this year also Messrs. Green, Wigrams and Green, as the firm was now styled, began to take an interest in the whaling trade, and for this purpose purchased the "Matilda," and in the following year they launched for themselves the "Harpooner," of 374 tons.

1830.   In 1830 occurred the great shipwright's strike, which will long be remembered by those connected with shipping on the River Thames. This strike lasted so long, that the grass is said to have grown up in the building slips, and the foremen and apprentices, who were almost the only people in the yard, were required by Mr. Green to work together on any jobs that might happen to come in. It was during this strike that Nathaniel Clarke, a very leading man among the shipwrights, first came prominently into notice. Mr. Green was so much struck with his ability, that taking him aside, he offered him at once the post of foreman, and another well-known foreman shipwright, Thomas Gaster, received his promotion about the same time under somewhat similar circumstances. The shipwrights were ultimately successful in their strike, and their Union dates from this period. The East India ships, in which the firm now held an interest, were the "Duke of York," "Repulse," "Sir David Scott," "Fairlee," "Atlas," "Lady Melville," "Minerva," "Marchioness of Ely," Prince Regent," "Rose," &c. It will have been observed that the building of large ships for the East India Company's service had by this time ceased, in view of the looked for expiration of their trading charter. Individual firms, however, had been gradually preparing themselves to compete with private enterprise for those valuable eastern trades, which for so many years had been conducted almost exclusively under the East India Company's direction. The Blackwall firm undoubtedly was in a very good position to avail itself fully of this opportunity, and for the next few years we find it chiefly occupied in purchasing or building vessels, either for the interests of the firm collectively, or for the different partners. The first ship owned by Mr. Wigram, as a separate venture, was the "Mary," of 300 tons, purchased by him this year, and commanded by Captain Henry Shuttleworth, now an elder brother of the Trinity House ; this ship was subsequently wrecked in Mossel Bay; the

" Lady Nugent " and the " Jane " were also purchased at this time by Mr. Wigram.

1831. On January the 1st, 1831, the " Euretta," of 335 tons, was launched, and on March 30th Henry Green became a partner in the business at the age of twenty-three, when the shares were held as follows : George Green, two-twelfths; Money Wigram, three-twelfths; Henry Loftus Wigram, three-twelfths : Richard Green, two-twelfths ; and Henry Green, two-twelfths. On the 14th of April, the " Duke of Buccleugh," of 576 tons, was launched for George Green, Esq., and on August 29th, another whaling ship, the " Vigilant," of 383 tons, was launched for the firm.

1832. On May 14th the " London," of 577 tons, was launched for Money Wigram, Esq., and this ship may be considered as the real pioneer of Messrs. Money Wigram and Son's fine fleet of passenger vessels. The " Prince Regent," of 992 tons, was also purchased by the firm, and in this year Mr. Green's second daughter, Mrs. Britten, was married from the Yard.

1833. The year 1833 will be ever memorable in the annals of our merchant shipping as being that in which the East India Company's Charter ceased, and the trade to the East was thrown open to private enterprise ; an immediate impetus was naturally given to the so called free traders, and before very long the passenger vessels belonging to Messrs. Green and Wigram, Messrs. T. & W. Smith, Messrs. Duncan Dunbar and Co., Messrs. Somes and others, began to be recognised as filling to a large extent the place which had heretofore been occupied by the vessels of the East India Company.

The " Carnatic," of 598 tons, was launched for George Green, Esq., and the whaler " Eleanor," for Messrs. Green, Wigrams & Green. The paddle-wheel steamer " Monarch," of 856 tons, was also launched for the London and Edinboro' Steam Packet Company, and was commanded by Captain Bain, whose son, the present Dr. Bain, has for many years been known as one of the leading practitioners in the East of London. This steamer was at once taken up, with several other vessels, to carry volunteers to Portugal in support of Don Pedro in his contest with Don Miguel. The volunteers on board the " Monarch " having been recruited largely from the Isle of Dogs and its neighbourhood, became known familiarly in the expedition as the " Isle of Dogians."

1834. The " Malabar," of 603 tons, was launched for George Green, Esq., the " Eagle," of 362 tons, for Money Wigram, Esq., and the " Narwhal," whaler of 370 tons, for the firm. The " Alexander Baring," of 478 tons,

H 1

was also launched for the well known firm of Baring Brothers. On October the 1st, 1834, Mr. Henry Green was married, and on this interesting occasion, a grand ball was given in the mould loft, which was handsomely decorated for the occasion, to the principal friends and inhabitants of the neighbourhood. The few survivors of that day still speak in terms of admiration of the gaiety and pleasure of the entertainment. Mr. Henry Green, after his marriage lived in the house in the middle of the Yard, which had for some years previously been occupied by Mr. H. L. Wigram, and he continued to reside there, where his six elder children were born, until the Yard was divided in 1843, Mr. H. L. Wigram moving to the smaller house adjoining the entrance gates. The large house was at this time still occupied by Mr. George Green's family.

1835.   In this year a still further curtailment was made in the size of Messrs. Green's and Wigram's ship-yard, which at this time was still spoken of as "the most considerable private concern in Europe," by the sale of land to the Blackwall Railway Company, which had just been formed. Until this time the boundaries of the yard had for many years extended from the river Thames northwards to Naval Row, and from Brunswick Street eastwards to the East India Dock. Among the large piles of oak timber and planking, wild rabbits still made themselves at home, and not many years before, fine salmon had been taken off the Yard; now, however, the River at this part had come to be generally recognized as the head quarters of the whitebait, which were caught at Blackwall in large quantities, and could, as it was said, be enjoyed only to perfection if eaten at the Artichoke or Brunswick Taverns. The northern part of the Yard was then an open field where Mr. George Green's cows and horses used to graze, and where his favourite old horse, "Playfellow," is buried just behind the Masthouse. In the middle of the yard was the large timber-pond and wet-dock, spoken of by Pepys' in 1665 : this was partially filled in when the Blackwall Railway was constructed, and was reduced again when after 1843 extensive saw-mills were erected on the site by Messrs. Wigrams, it was finally filled in by these gentlemen, and turned into a building-slip for the construction of Her Majesty's fine Indian troop-ship, "Crocodile." The "True Briton," of 646 tons, was launched for Money Wigram, Esq., and kept up the recollection of Sir Robert Wigram's early venture. The "Windsor," of 656 tons, was launched for George Green, Esq., and the paddle-wheel steamers, "Beaver" and "Columbia," of 188 tons, for the Hudson's Bay Company.

1836.   The "Slain's Castle," of 375 tons, was launched for Money Wigram,

Esq., and the "Walmer Castle," of 620 tons, for George Green, Esq.; the paddle-wheel steamers, "Caledonia," of 571 tons, and "Atalanta," of 606 tons, for the Edinboro' Steam Packet Company. The paddle-wheel steamers, "Countess of Lonsdale," of 621 tons, and the "Clarence," of 737 tons, for the General Steam Navigation Company, and the "Antonio Pereira," opium clipper, for Captain W. O. Young. This vessel unfortunately capsized into the river while launching.

1837.   This year the "Seringapatam," of 818 tons, was launched for Richard Green, Esq. This ship was again the first of a new class, and was a great advance in size and form on previous vessels ; in her the double stern and galleries were abandoned, which at the time was looked upon as an important stride. She had a figure head of "Tippoo Sahib" painted in proper colours, with a drawn scimitar in hand. This was a never failing source of delight to the natives in Calcutta, who used to raise their oars in passing, and look with admiration at old Tippoo, exclaiming—"Wha wha, bhote atcha," (very good, very good). The old "Sering," as she was generally called, was always noted for her quick and regular passages, and became the model for many succeeding vessels. She was commanded on her first voyage by Captain George Denny, and afterwards by Captain James Furnell, who subsequently became the Superintendent of the Sailor's Home, where he remained for many years until his death in 1878. The "Madagascar," of 835 tons, was also launched for Richard Green, Esq., and was commanded by Captain W. H. Walker, afterwards Sir W. H. Walker, of the Board of Trade. The "Emu," 293 tons, was launched for Money Wigram, Esq.; this vessel had been designed for the newly opening trade to Australia, for which purpose she was then considered very well adapted. The whaler, "Active," of 461 tons, was launched for the firm, the steamer "Neptune," of 621 tons, for the General Steam Navigation Company, and the steamer "Madagascar," of 351 tons, for the Portuguese Government.

1838.   In this year Mr. George Green retired from active business. The "Earl of Hardwicke," of 852 tons, was launched for Richard Green, Esq., and commanded by Captain Alexander Henning, R.N., and in the following
1839. year her sister ships, the "Vernon" and "Owen Glendower," were launched for the same owners. The "Earl of Hardwicke" and "Vernon" were fitted with auxilliary steam-side paddles, of 100 horse-power, to be used during calms. This arrangement, however, did not prove successful, and was soon removed. The "Owen Glendower," which was considered a remarkably handsome vessel, had painted on the front of her poop—"I can call spirits

from the vasty deep;" she was for many years commanded by Captain William Toller. To this ship, and for several years before and afterwards, to all these splendid frigate-built vessels, foreign merchantmen were in the habit of lowering their top-sails as if to ships of war.

The " Essex," of 851 tons, and the " Maidstone," of 819 tons, were launched by Money Wigram, Esq., and the opium clipper "Moa." for Messrs. Jardine, Matheson & Co.

1840.

The " Tartar " and " Samarang," of 454 tons, were launched for the firm, the " Vancouver " and " Cowlitz," of 286 tons, for the Hudson's Bay Company, and three new light vessels for the Trinity Corporation.

1841.

The " Prince Albert " and " Prince Rupert," each of 286 tons, were launched for the Hudson's Bay Company. The " Caroline," of 323 tons, for Messrs. Thomson, Hankey & Co., and the paddle-wheel steamer " Princess Royal," of 666 tons, and the " Trident," of 875 tons, for the General Steam Navigation Company. The " Trident " was at this time considered one of the fastest vessels afloat, and on Queen Victoria's first visit to Scotland, she so far passed in speed the Royal Yacht, that the " Trident " was chartered for Her Majesty's party on the return voyage.

In this year also, the sister ships " Agincourt " and " Southampton," of 852 tons, were launched respectively for Richard Green and Money Wigram, Esqrs. It will have been observed by this time, that for the last few years the interests of the partners in the new ships they were building for themselves, had more and more become divided, and in this year, 1841, the only vessels owned by them in common were the " Pyramus " and " Roxburgh Castle."

1842.

The " Malacca," of 491 tons, was launched for Richard Green, Esq., and the paddle steamer " Montezuma," of 1,080 tons, for the Mexican Government, under the supervision of Messrs. Lizardi & Co. This year also the magnificent flush-deck, frigate-built sister ships " Queen " and " Prince of Wales," of 1,223 tons, were built—one for the Messrs. Wigrams, and the other for the Messrs. Greens. The " Sylph," of 449 tons, was launched for Messrs. T. Daniels & Company, and this was the last ship ever launched by the firm of Green, Wigrams & Green.

1843.

In 1843, a year ever memorable in the history of Blackwall the term of partnership expired, and it was deemed advisable to terminate the old connection, and to divide the Yard and ships : the cause of this division may be roughly traced to the distinct and even differing interests which had been created by the families each owning separate vessels. The division of the

Yard being settled on, the western portion with the house and entrance was made over to the newly created firm of Messrs. Money, Wigram and Sons, and the eastern portion with a sum of money and another entrance was apportioned to that of Messrs. Richard and Henry Green. A captain who had served under the old firm for many years describes his feelings of distress, when on returning home, he found "a brick wall running through the Yard and the red cross through the flag."

In concluding this portion of our Chronicles, it will hardly be deemed out of place, if some further particulars are given of the life of Mr. George Green, who for more than sixty years had been so closely identified with Blackwall Yard and the surrounding neighbourhood.*

George Green was born at Cheshunt, in Hertfordshire, on November 2nd, 1767. He was the second son of Mr. John Green, a well-known brewer at Chelsea, and of Mary Pritzler, his wife; his only brother John was lost at sea in early life, and his only sister Mary, who was born in 1769, became in 1799 the second wife of Mr. John Perry of Blackwall. For many years the Green family had been prominently connected with Chelsea, and for several generations they had owned considerable property in that parish. For more than a century Green's brewery appears to have been one of the leading institutions of the neighbourhood, and various references are made to it and to the family in Faulkner's History of Chelsea.

Before the year 1682 the Government had purchased land near the river from Mr. John Green, the great grandfather of George Green, which land afterwards formed part of the site on which Chelsea Hospital was built. About the year 1716 Mrs. Elizabeth Green, then a widow, died, leaving her estate in Chelsea to her son Thomas, who in 1708 had married Mary Rose, and afterwards Frances Atherton. By the first marriage he left an only daughter, Elizabeth, to whom he bequeathed his fortune on condition that her husband, Edward Burnaby, a brother of Admiral Sir William Burnaby, should assume the name of Green. In 1740 Thomas Green died. Edward Burnaby and Elizabeth Green had a son Charles, who, at his death, left his property to his son, Pitt Burnaby Green, a Lieutenant in the Royal Navy. Pitt Burnaby appears to have then retired from his profession and joined

---

* A very good account of Blackwall Yard at this time is given in a book entitled "Days at the Factories," published by Charles Knight and Co., 1843.

the Brewery, in partnership with his relations, John and Richard Green. In the year 1760 the "Annual Register" in its "History of the London Brewery," gives an account of the quantity of beer which had been brewed at the principal brew-houses from Midsummer, 1759, to Midsummer, 1760, by which it appears that Green's Brewery had supplied 9,770 barrels. About twelve years after this time, however, a change appears to have come over the good fortunes of the business.

John Green, who is said to have been an extravagant man, and fonder of driving his four-in-hand than of managing his business, could hardly have found a much more practical partner in his nephew the Lieutenant, who was chiefly known as the possessor of a valuable library, and as the author of several poetical works; it is by no means surprising, therefore, to find that in 1772 the firm had become involved in serious difficulties. On May 29th of the same year, John Green died rather suddenly, and before the year had closed, the estate was wound up in bankruptcy. On the death of her husband Mrs. Green went with her two young children, George and Mary, to reside at Battersea, and in the year 1782, George Green, then fifteen years of age, was, through the instrumentality of his aunt, Mrs. Pritzler, introduced to Blackwall Yard, where he was apprenticed to Mr. Perry. He is spoken of at this time as having been particularly active, intelligent, and trustworthy, and he soon began to make himself useful in the drawing-office and mould loft, where he was employed in designing and laying of ships. A proof of his activity is given in the fact that for some time he was in the habit of frequently walking from his mother's house, near Battersea, to Blackwall Yard, arriving there at six o'clock in the morning and walking back again after six o'clock in the evening. In the busy times that were now coming on, George Green was frequently detained at the Yard until late in the evening, working in the mould loft, and at such times Mr. Perry and his family would often walk through from the adjoining house to see how things were going on. Report says, further, that Miss Sarah Perry took a somewhat lively interest in these proceedings, and would show her interest by rubbing out and otherwise disturbing the lines which young George Green had just completed. However this may be an attachment soon sprang up between them, they became engaged, and were married at St. Dunstan's, Stepney, on February 18th, 1796. In the following year George Green was taken into partnership at the age of thirty. Five children were born of this marriage, John, George, Joseph, Mary, and Richard. Of these, Joseph and Mary died in infancy.

On May 18th, 1805, Mrs. George Green died at the age of twenty-eight, and the day following her eldest son John died at the age of nine years. Frequently, in after years, Mr. Green would describe his feelings of grief and loneliness at this time when his wife and eldest son were both lying dead together in the house.

On May 6th, 1806, Mr. Green married for his second wife Elizabeth, daughter of William Unwin, Esq., of Bromley and Sawbridgeworth; by this marriage he had six children, Henry, Elizabeth, Emma, Clara, Frederick, and William. Of these Clara died in 1814 from the results of an accident, and in the same year her half-brother George, described as a boy of good promise, died at Brighton, at the age of fifteen, from the effects of bathing while heated after riding. Richard was now the only surviving child of Mr. Green's first marriage, and it was possibly on this account that he was always regarded by his father with peculiar affection and solicitude. It is interesting now to remember that Richard and his brother Henry were in 1816 at Doctor Cogan's school, at Higham Hill, Walthamstow; among their schoolfellows were Benjamin Disraeli (Earl Beaconsfield), Russell Gurney, the late Recorder of London, Samuel Solly, F.R.S., Gilbert Macmurdo and Benjamin Travers, who became distinguished as surgeons, with many others whose names have since become known to the world. At this time Mr. Green was residing in the large house in Blackwall Yard, which had previously been occupied by Mr. Perry. There is nothing especially to record of him at this period, except that he was unremitting in his attention to business, and expected all around him to be the same. He was always an early riser, and took steps to instil the same good habit into his children. He was generally to be seen riding on his cob before six o'clock in the morning, and if he did not always succeed in getting his children to ride with him at this early hour, he successfully encouraged them to take a delight in this healthful exercise, and there are still some living at Blackwall who can remember his daughters who were admirable horse-women, exercising their horses round the large field behind the mast-house. Mr. Green's naturally kind and benevolent disposition was continually shown in many ways towards those among whom he lived: one of his most intimate friends, and a constant visitor at Blackwall, was his cousin Colonel Pritzler, afterwards General Sir Theophilus Pritzler, and it was always a subject of much satisfaction to Mr. Green to find himself in a position to repay in some measure the kindness and assistance which he had received in early days from his aunt, Mrs. Pritzler, and other members

I

of this family. No influence had probably more shaped his character and course of life than the example and advice of Mr. Perry, for whose memory he entertained to the last moment feelings of the deepest affection and esteem.

In the year 1815 Mr. Green, who had for some time been much impressed with the scarce and quite inadequate means of education which were afforded for the children of the neighbourhood, took a leading part in promoting the erection of the " Poplar and Blackwall Free School," which was designed for the education of " at least 300 boys and 200 girls," these children were all to be clothed, and the rules most carefully prescribed that religious as well as secular teaching should at all times be strictly attended to. The Honourable East India Company, the West India Dock Company, the East India Dock Company, Messrs. Wigrams and Green, together with most of the leading inhabitants of the neighbourhood, responded liberally to the appeal which Mr. Green, as treasurer, had made on behalf of the schools. They were opened in the following year by His Royal Highness the Duke of Kent, accompanied by the Bishop of Norwich and other distinguished persons. Towards the maintenance of these Schools Mr. Green at once contributed a handsome endowment, and to the last retained an especial interest in this, the first of those larger philanthropic schemes by which he was continually seeking to benefit those around him. Among those associated with Mr. Green in this good work as trustees, subscribers, or members of the managing committee, were his friends Messrs. Leonard Currie, George Frederick Young, William Melluish, John Garford, John Stock, Robert Batson, William Sims, John Montague, and others. The Poplar and Blackwall Free School was maintained in a most efficient state down to the year 1874, when, for various reasons, it was deemed advisable that a general meeting of the supporters of these schools should be called, in order to consider their position with regard to the newly-formed School Board for London. It was then agreed—" That taking into consideration the altered circumstances of elementary education since these Schools were founded, it is expedient that the management of the ' The Poplar and Blackwall Free Schools ' be now transferred to the School Board for London." This resolution was put into effect, and the Endowment Fund was handed over to the Charity Commissioners with a request that, to carry out the spirit of the founders, these funds might be devoted to the furtherance of religious instruction among certain of the most important schools in the neighbourhood.

The schools have since been entirely rebuilt, and are now known as the "Woolmore Street Board Schools."

In 1818 Mr. Green purchased the Grosvenor House estate at Walthamstow, where he resided however only for a short time. In 1821 he followed the example of Sir Henry Johnson, and built twelve almshouses, adjoining the Yard, for the benefit of old and infirm workmen who had faithfully served the firm. These houses received the appropriate name of "Shipwrights Terrace."

In 1828 Mr. George Green's mother, Mrs. John Green, died, at the age of eighty-eight years, and was buried in Poplar Chapel. This year Mr. Green commenced to build another large school in the East India Road, known as the "Chrisp Street School." This was subsequently enlarged for the accommodation of 120 boys and 250 girls.

The Chrisp Street School, which was very largely endowed, was, during Mr. Green's lifetime, managed almost entirely under his own directions, by a committee, consisting of his daughters Mrs. Hankey and Mrs. Britten, his daughters-in-law Mrs. Henry Green and Mrs. Frederick Green, his niece Miss Perry, and several others. At the present time the school is working well under a committee similarly constituted, and affords a good education to the numerous children of the locality. In 1833 Mr. Green built and endowed the large infant school at the corner of Preston's Road, where children are taught in connection with the Chrisp Street School.

At this time Mr. Green was residing chiefly at Clapham, where he had purchased a house, and from here his eldest daughter, Elizabeth, was married to Mr. Thomas Hankey, on June 22nd, 1831.

In 1836 Mr. Green's third son Frederick, who after an extended tour in the East, had been for some little time in the office of Sir John Pirie and Co., was placed in business with Captain W. Tucker, who had previously commanded the "Lady Raffles," as ship and insurance brokers, at 64, Cornhill. The style of the new firm was F. Green and Co., and they then undertook the loading and brokerage business of Messrs. Green's ships, which they have continued ever since. About the year 1840 Mr. Green's fourth son William took his degree at Oxford, and was ordained to a curacy in Derbyshire, under the Rev. Walter Shirley, afterwards Bishop of Sodor and Man. The Rev. William Green became subsequently Rector of Penshurst, Kent.

In 1841 Mr. Green built the well-known Sailor's Home in the East India Road for the benefit of the officers and seamen of his own vessels.

I I

This Home, which was one of the first and best-known institutions of the sort, was for many years ably conducted by Captains Furnell and Dunlop, who had commanded ships in Messrs. Green's service, and were thoroughly competent to carry out the benevolent designs of the founder. It may be stated, however, that although this Home was maintained by Mr. Green, and after his death by his son Mr. Richard Green, it never paid its own expenses, owing probably to the too expensive scale on which it had been originated. After the death of Mr. Richard Green the Home passed under the management of the Board of Trade, when it ceased to be used for its original purpose, and was re-arranged as a shipping-office for engaging and paying off crews.

In this year also Mr. Green built the large schools in North Street for the benefit of the children connected with Trinity Chapel. These Schools have within the last few years been handed over, like the Poplar and Blackwall Free Schools, to the management of the School Board for London.

In 1842 Mr. Green, who about this time appears to have left the Church of England, built Trinity Chapel, in the East India Road, together with a convenient parsonage, and an endowment. He also built a row of almshouses in North Street, looking on to the burial ground of Trinity Chapel, for the benefit of the old members of the congregations attending Trinity Chapel, Poplar Chapel, and Cotton Street Chapel, and to provide for the maintenance of these Almshouses he built Trinity Terrace, adjoining to Trinity Chapel, the rents from which are appropriated for the due maintenance of the Almshouses, and for the benefit of the inhabitants. In 1844 Mr. Green purchased three houses adjoining to the Chrisp Street School, in order to convert them into residences for the master and mistress.

On November 2nd, 1846, Mrs. Green died at the age of sixty-nine years.

In 1847 Mr. Green purchased a large building in Bow Lane, and adapted this for a school. The extraordinary zeal and munificence which Mr. Green had shown for so many years in building and endowing schools, and in other acts of charity, on which he expended over one hundred thousand pounds, was at this time publicly recognised by a request that he would allow his portrait to be painted for the Town Hall, and from this portrait the accompanying engraving has been sketched. On February 21st, 1849, Mr. Green died at Blackwall in the eighty-second year of his age, and was buried in a vault attached to Trinity Chapel.

In respect for his memory the shops throughout the neighbourhood were closed, and the entire population seemed to line the road ; the flags on all the ships in the adjoining docks were half-mast high, and the procession seemed in every way to partake of the nature of a public funeral.   A handsome monument was soon afterwards erected to his memory by the workmen of Blackwall Yard.   The site was appropriately chosen, and the intimate connection which had existed for so many years between the East India Company and the Dockyard was recognised once more when George Green's monument was placed with those of Henry Johnson and John Perry in the East India Company's Chapel, which Sir Henry had assisted to erect, and with which the Perrys and George Green had been so long associated.

End of Part I.